THE SPANISH CIVIL WAR

Domestic Crisis or International Conspiracy?

PROBLEMS IN EUROPEAN CIVILIZATION

THE
SPANISH CIVIL WAR

Domestic Crisis or
International Conspiracy?

EDITED WITH AN INTRODUCTION BY

Gabriel Jackson

UNIVERSITY OF CALIFORNIA, SAN DIEGO

D. C. HEATH AND COMPANY · BOSTON

Englewood · Indianopolis · Dallas · Burlingame · Atlanta

Table of Contents

Introduction

THE SPANISH CIVIL WAR began on July 18, 1936 as a revolt on the part of the professional military against the civilian republican regime. Such military risings had been frequent in nineteenth-century Spain. They had indeed given international currency to the Spanish word *pronunciamiento,* meaning a relatively bloodless military overthrow of the existing government. But the revolt of the generals in July, 1936 turned out to be far more than another *pronunciamiento.* In the course of the ensuing two and one half years well over 1,000,000 Spaniards (out of a population totalling about 27,000,000) took up arms against each other. Neither side could prevail without foreign aid. The Republican cause depended heavily upon Russian armaments, aviators, tank drivers, and staff officers. Between thirty and forty thousand anti-fascist volunteers, flocking to Spain against the will of their governments, fought in the Republican ranks. The forces under General Francisco Franco, known variously as Insurgents and as Nationalists, depended increasingly throughout the war on the armed aid of Italy, Germany, and Portugal. Upwards of 70,000 Italians, and perhaps 20,000 Portuguese fought in the Nationalist ranks, while the Germans supplied several thousand technical specialists. Public opinion in all the countries of Europe and the Western hemisphere was passionately divided as to the political and moral issues involved in the struggle. All major European governments strove to influence the outcome of the war, and all of them feared the possibility, while the fighting continued, that the Spanish Civil War might "escalate" into a fullscale European war.

However, the international ramifications of the war should not lead the student to neglect its importance as a critical event in the history of the Spanish people. The outcome of the war was determined by foreign intervention. But Spain, with her careful policy of neutrality in the main international quarrels of the twentieth century, could hardly have become the victim of foreign intervention, whether fascist or communist in inspiration, if she had not been sorely divided against herself as a nation. It is therefore necessary to judge all literature concerning the Civil War against a background of the internal problems of Spain.

Every society must rest upon certain assumptions which command at least the passive consent, if not the conscious loyalty, of the majority of its citizens. In Spain as a whole, until the middle of the nineteenth century, and in Spain outside the few great cities until at least 1914, the accepted form of government was monarchy, the accepted religion was that embodied in the Roman Catholic Church as an established Church, and the dominant form of agricultural life in southern Spain consisted of large landed estates cultivated rather inefficiently by landless laborers who were paid absolutely minimal wages. Direct military government was the exception rather than the rule, but the Army distinctly considered itself the corporate guardian of essential national interests, and its frequent interference in politics was an accepted fact of life. The business and professional middle classes were relatively small. They lacked self-confidence in politics and, therefore, left the control of public affairs pretty much in the hands of the landed aristocracy. The small industrial working class was capable of great militance at particular moments, concerning particular issues; but ideologically the workers were very much divided. On the whole they lacked both the consistent organization and the educated leadership necessary for effective participation in politics.

During the first three decades of the twentieth century these several assumptions were increasingly called into question. The urban population became largely republican or, at the very least, ceased to feel any traditional respect or affection for the monarchy. The city dwellers, the landless proletariat of southern Spain, the miners and industrial workers, became increasingly skeptical in their religious outlook and hostile to the Catholic Church as an established Church. Large numbers of landless workers from the poor provinces of southern Spain migrated to the industrial districts of Catalonia, and those who remained behind were increasingly restive under the conditions of near-serfdom prevailing on the great estates. Military interference in politics during the long drawn out Moroccan "pacification" (c. 1909–1927) became increasingly aggressive and decidedly less acceptable to public opinion than in the mid-nineteenth century. Industrial workers, hearing of the Russian Revolution of 1917 and of the Italian factory occupations of 1919, turned increasingly to "direct action" tactics in immediate industrial struggles and to thoughts of a thoroughgoing social revolution in the proximate future.

These political and social problems were further complicated by the development of strong local autonomy movements in Catalonia and the Basque provinces. Both areas possessed a distinctive language and a long cultural history of their own. Both were more prosperous, more industrial, more "European" minded than Castile. Both were dissatisfied with a central government dominated by agrarian and military interests. The Army in its turn regarded the Catalan and Basque autonomy movements as subversive and "anti-national."

By the time of the First World War the traditional framework of society was falling apart. Theoretically Spain was a constitutional monarchy, but by 1917 even fixed elections could no longer produce stable majorities. Supposedly all Spaniards were Catholics, but only peasant and middle-class women practiced their religion with any regularity. The Army, traditionally the repository of Spanish honor, broke strikes at home and could not complete the pacification of Morocco. That Army saved its "honor" and the King saved his throne by resort to outright military dictatorship in 1923. In 1930 the world depression and the accumulated disgust of most articulate Spaniards brought the dictatorship to an end. The following year, when municipal elections returned republican majorities in the large cities, the King departed, not officially abdicating but clearly acknowledging the adverse judgment of the Spanish people with regard to his personal reign.

For two years the new parliamentary Republic was governed by a coalition of Republicans and Socialists. This coalition, under the leadership of Manuel Azaña, initiated a broad range of reforms. It decreed the separation of Church and State, enacted Spain's first divorce law, and began the rapid expansion of the secular public school system while demanding that Church-run primary schools cease to function after a transition period of about two years. All this was done in a frankly anticlerical spirit, the Roman Catholic Church being looked upon as an enemy of free thought and as the unjustified possessor of monopoly rights in the fields of religion and education. The government also reduced the size of the Army, and Cortes discussions of the military very much wounded the pride of the officer caste. Public works programs, and indeed the mere participation of Socialists in the cabinet, placed the new regime at odds with the industrial and financial oligarchy. Plans for compensated land reform, even though very gradualist in conception, placed the landlord class in opposition. The Statute of Autonomy granted to Catalonia aroused the fears of conservative nationalists. At the same time that the new government was challenging the traditional ruling elements of Spain, the anarchists preached a quick transition from the Republic to *comunismo libertario* (economic communism without centralized political control of the Soviet type) and tried to hasten that transition by revolutionary strikes leading to clashes with the police and the traditionally hated Civil Guards.

The rapid reform program of the Republican-Socialist coalition bogged down in the summer of 1933. Parliamentary elections in November of that year brought to power a new coalition of conservative and clerical parties. For the next two years the government tried essentially to reverse the reform program. Land distribution came virtually to a halt. Church schools regained their privileged standing. The structural reform of the Army was maintained, while the attitude of the government emphasized traditional religion and "law and order." To the liberals and the Left, the Spain of 1933–35 appeared simply to be the corrupt, conservative monarchy without the person of the King.

During the years 1931–35 as a whole, no new forms of loyalty or passive acceptance developed to replace the assumptions on which Spanish society had depended in the nineteenth century. The Left was disgruntled by its inability to reform Spain in a few years by legislative fiat. The Right demanded a return to the *status quo ante* without offering any constructive solutions for the longstanding ills of the nation. In these circumstances Spaniards of all classes and viewpoints became increasingly restive, uncertain of their relation to each other, and ready to resort to violence.

In October 1934, a divided and fearful Left rose against a government which seemed to be drifting in the direction of clerical fascism such as had developed in Austria under Chancellor Dollfuss. General strikes in Madrid and several other cities failed. In Barcelona the regional government, under the pressure of Catalan nationalists, declared Spain to be a "federal" republic. The movement was defeated in one night, and with comparatively little bloodshed. But in the northern province of Asturias, armed miners established revolutionary committees composed of Socialist, Communist, and Anarchist delegates. Despite the failure of the movement elsewhere in Spain, the miners invaded the provincial capital, Oviedo, and fought for two weeks against the police and the Moorish and Foreign Legion troops brought from Morocco to suppress the insurrection.

The class and ideological confrontations in Asturias prefigured those of the Civil War. The brutal repression, and the holding of thousands of political prisoners throughout 1935, deepened the hatreds which had found expression in the fighting itself. A little more than a year later, the elections of February, 1936 polarized the population into two mutually fearful coalitions of almost equal strength. The Left coalition, known as the Popular Front, included all shades of opinion from moderate secular liberals to Communists and Anarchists, with its main numerical strength being constituted by the Socialists. The Right coalition included all shades of opinion from conservative republican to monarchist and fascist, with its main numerical strength consisting of the Catholic middle class of Spain as a whole and the bulk of the peasantry of northern Spain.

The fears and rivalries within each coalition were more powerful than the minimum bases of unity around which they had been formed. In the spring of 1936 centrifugal forces seemed literally to be dismantling the state. No single leader or party possessed sufficient prestige to achieve a truce among the competing fragments of the Spanish body politic. During this same season high officers of the Army were planning the *pronunciamiento* which was launched on July 18. Its leaders doubtless hoped that, as in the nineteenth century, or as in September, 1923, politically conscious Army officers would rout the "incompetent" politicians and form a government that would save Spain from "chaos." But neither the liberal middle class, nor the industrial working class, nor a large proportion of the peasantry, nor the Catalan and Basque autonomists, would accept a military government on this occasion. Within a few days the unsuccessful *pronunciamiento* had been transformed into the thirty-three month struggle known to the world as the Spanish Civil War.

Like all revolutionary upheavals, the Spanish Civil War was very differently interpreted by different sorts of participants. Middle-class liberals thought of themselves as defending the civilian parliamentary regime against the threat of military dictatorship. Anticlericals fought to destroy the institutional power of the Catholic Church. Anarchist peasants and factory workers saw an opportunity to establish *comunismo libertario*: a decentralized, collectivist, proletarian-controlled form of economy. The Spanish Communist Party, like all the world Communist parties in the years 1935–39, pursued the policy of a "Popular Front." In the face of the Hitlerite threat to both the Soviet Union and Western democracy, they urged the active cooperation of all democratic and Left anti-fascist forces. Within wartime Republican Spain this meant postponing indefinitely the socialist revolution, conciliating property owners, and working with middle-class liberals and moderate Socialists to establish a regime that would win the confidence and the backing of the Western Powers. On the other hand, the radical Socialists of Largo Caballero, and the small but influential anti-Stalinist Marxist party in Catalonia, the POUM, saw in the war a unique opportunity to carry through the socialist revolution without creating a bureaucratic dictatorship such as that of Stalin. These sharp differences of belief as to the significance of the Civil War undermined the unity of the Republican defense. In May, 1937,

these differences were a prime cause of the several days' street fighting in Barcelona between the partisans of the Stalinist and the anti-Stalinist Left.

In the Nationalist zone peasant and middle class Catholics rose to defend the Church against the threat of "atheism" and "communism." Part of the officer corps fought for a military dictatorship of the traditional type, and others dreamed of a regime similar in many respects to those of the dominant fascist powers Italy and Germany. International opinion identified these various Spanish forces with the dominant political forces struggling throughout the European world. Proletarian forces under one form or another of anarchist or Marxist leadership were lumped together under the heading "Communist." Parliamentary and anticlerical forces were identified with "democracy." Clerical, royalist, and military forces were identified with "fascism."

The war lasted for almost three years, in part because of the passionate sense of involvement among the Spanish people as a whole, in part because of the nature of international intervention in the struggle. During the weekend of July 17–20, 1936, the populations of the key cities of Madrid and Barcelona defeated the *pronunciamiento* while the civilian government hesitated in its attitude towards the rebellious officers. Throughout the war the Republican army lacked armament and professional officers, but made up in enthusiasm and sacrifice what it lacked in equipment. At the same time, all the intervening powers tried to limit their commitment as much as possible. For the Soviets the shipment of arms through the Mediterranean Sea was dangerous and costly. In supporting the Insurgents or Nationalists, Italy and Germany had originally counted upon a very short war — several months at most. Only grudgingly did they extend to General Franco the massive support that was necessary to overcome the resistance of the great majority of the Spanish people.

When the war ended in April, 1939, several hundred thousand Spaniards and tens of thousands of foreign soldiers had died. General Francisco Franco had achieved total military and political control of Spain, a control which he was to maintain for a full quarter century thereafter. Internally, his victory represented the triumph of the conservative forces whose traditional power had been increasingly challenged from the nineteenth century until July, 1936: the Army, the Church, the landed aristocracy and its allies in the world of business and industry. In the international context his victory represented a major triumph for the fascist powers, a triumph comparable in significance to the Italian victory over Ethiopia in 1936 and the German dismemberment of Czechoslovakia in 1938. The Nationalist victory had also been achieved, in large measure, through the nonintervention policy of the major European powers, a policy which had prevented the Republic from buying arms while the Nationalists were heavily supplied by Germany and Italy. In this regard the victory of General Franco was a victory for the political groups within England and France which in the years 1935–39 favored "appeasement" of the fascist powers. It was also a decisive defeat for the Communist-sponsored policy of the Popular Front and "collective security" against fascism.

This set of readings is designed to introduce the student to the complex perspectives and viewpoints involved in the Spanish Civil War. Obviously the title question "Domestic Crisis or International Conspiracy?" cannot be answered in a categorical fashion one way or the other. The reader will frequently be aware of the interaction between internal Spanish conditions and the international developments preceding the Second World War. But the editorial division is based on the conviction that there is no better way to approach an understanding of the Spanish Civil War than to ask oneself at all points: how much of the conflict is attributable to internal conditions, and how much to international power politics and international ideological struggles? The readings are thus divided into one group dealing primarily with domestic conditions and developments, and a second dealing primarily with the international aspects of the Civil War. The range of viewpoints among the authors chosen is very wide. They vary not only as to domestic *vs.* international emphasis. They have very different emotional sympathies and very different views as to the relative importance of economic, ideological and personal factors in the events they describe. Nevertheless, there are certain focal questions which can be asked of all the readings. Would the Civil War have occurred if fascism had not previously triumphed in Italy and Germany? Was communism, domestic and/or international, a major cause of the Civil War? Would the struggle have broken out if the government had been able to control the Anarchists? If it had been able to control the Falange? Would Civil War have been avoidable if the clerical issue had been more wisely handled? In the case of the many "disorders," who initiated the violence, and with what motives? Finally, does serious civil conflict place a small nation at the mercy of powers who choose to exploit that conflict?

[NOTE: Footnotes have generally been omitted except where needed to explain the text.]

DEFINITIONS

The following initials and political terms appear repeatedly, particularly in the selections by Ramos Oliveira, Borkenau, and Orwell:

CEDA   Confederation of Autonomous Right parties, united in the defense of the Church and of private property, divided on the question of monarchy *vs.* republic.

CNT   the anarchist-led federation of trade unions.

ESQUERRA   Catalan liberal-left party, led by Luis Companys, espousing the autonomy statute, and the interests of small farmers and the lower middle class.

FAI   the Iberian Anarchist Federation, the core or elite leadership of the anarchist movement as a whole.

GENERALITAT   (spelled Generalidad in Castilian) the autonomous Catalan government, named after the medieval parliament of Aragon-Catalonia.

LLIGA CATALANA   conservative Catalan party, led by Francisco Cambó, representing big business and landlord interests.

POUM   revolutionary but anti-Stalinist Marxists, frequently labeled as "Trotskyites," but neither they nor the late Leon Trotsky considered the label accurate.

PSUC   the unified Socialist-Communist Party of Catalonia. The fusion occurred in the spring of 1936, and the party was clearly dominated by the Communists and "fellow-travelers."

UGT   the trade union federation associated with the Socialist Party.

The Conflict of Opinion

"During the last 130 years [c. 1812–1945] Spain has never known tranquillity. An unending tale of violence — *pronunciamientos* of every kind, terrorism, rebellion in the countryside, separatist movements — proclaimed on every occasion, even in the intervals when the military truce was in force, that the nation was living in a state of endemic civil war."

— A. Ramos Oliveira

"It was to prove the tragedy of the Republic that from the beginning its gravest dangers came precisely from the republican ranks."

— W. C. Atkinson

"On the battlefield of central Spain, today, the Comintern and the Fascintern are meeting in their first military battle; the course of history has involved the Spaniards, but the Spaniards are only auxiliaries."

— F. Borkenau

"The decisive factor in the war was, as has already been said, the foreign intervention. Germany and Italy supported the rebel generals from the start. Stalin only decided to intervene in September . . . The fascist dictators dealt directly with Franco and his generals . . . Stalin, on the other hand, saw to it that the arms which he supplied and the International Brigades which he organized should secure the predominance of the Communist Party."

— G. Brenan

I. THE DOMESTIC CRISIS OF THE 1930'S

Disillusion and Instability, 1898–1936

W. C. ATKINSON

W. C. Atkinson is a leading British authority on the literature of the entire Hispanic world and on the history specifically of Spain and Portugal. The following selection analyzes in some detail the political and social forces tending to undermine the stability of the Spanish monarchy after "the disaster of 1898," i.e., the Spanish-American War, which deprived Spain of her few remaining overseas colonies in the Caribbean and the Philippine Islands. Atkinson stresses particularly the conflicts between centralism and regionalism, between labor and the military, and between civilian and military authority. In order to place his factual account in proper perspective, the reader should note that he is almost equally critical of both conservative and liberal forces.

Some of the important questions raised by Atkinson's account are: What was the relation between the humiliation of the army in Morocco and the rise of Catalan nationalism? How did World War I contribute to the political decomposition of the monarchy? Why did Spain become a dictatorship in 1923? What were the main features of the Constitution of 1931? And why did the Republic fail to achieve stability between 1931 and 1936?

THE CHASTENED MOOD in which Spain entered the twentieth century did not prove in itself sufficient for regeneration. Inevitably, since no one could claim that the nation as a whole had yet been drawn into a responsible share in government, the disaster of 1898 was laid at the door of the politicians, to the further discrediting of politics. It was thus of particular ill-omen for the new reign that Alfonso XIII, declared of age at sixteen in May 1902 and formally sworn to observe the constitution, should have revealed himself from the beginning as much less a constitutional monarch or a statesman than as one politician more. Even had there been men immediately capable, like the Cánovas and Sagasta of the previous generation, of maintaining at least the semblance of continuity and tranquillity, the convention of conservative and liberal alternation in office had long since worn thin.

One reason was the emergence of new political forces, socialism and Catalanism in particular, that could not be accommodated within the two-party framework, with the consequent tendency to disintegration under new pressures of the two older groupings; another a growing resort to violence for political ends which often removed the struggle from Cortes to the streets. Of the notable political figures of this reign one of each major party, Dato and Canalejas, was eventually assassinated. Such political unease found early expression in the long series of cabinet crises and the eight prime ministers thrown up over the first four years, a period culminating

From W. C. Atkinson, *A History of Spain and Portugal* (Baltimore, 1960), pp. 320–331. Reprinted by permission of Penguin Books, Inc.

in the attempted murder of Alfonso himself on the day of his wedding in 1906 to an English princess, Victoria Eugenia.

Collapse of empire had not freed Spain entirely from overseas commitments and anxieties. There remained Africa. Spain's share in the general scramble over that continent had been limited to the acquisition between 1884 and 1886 of the barren wastes of Río de Oro, to the south-west of Morocco. After 1898 the national mood was all for retreat, not expansion; but the threatening disruption of the Moroccan empire shortly afterwards compelled a renewal of interest in that direction. The Anglo-French convention of 1904, basis of the Entente Cordiale, and the Algeciras conference of 1906 brought Spain with France into a general responsibility for Morocco, which the Franco-Spanish agreement of 1912 made explicit by establishing a Spanish protectorate over the north-western zone. This gave Spain both an Atlantic and a Mediterranean coastline in Africa and provided a substantial hinterland to the individual strongholds, from Ceuta to Melilla, which for centuries now had been under Spanish sovereignty.

Pacification of the zone added one more to the accumulating problems at home, where the unpopularity of service in Africa and the liberal denunciation of this "policy of conquest" provided constant scope for agitation. In 1909 tribal attacks on Melilla — the same spark that fired O'Donnell's war of 1859–60 — and the hurried despatch of reinforcements from Barcelona led to a major uprising, a general strike, and a death-roll of a hundred in the latter city. The execution in reprisal, among others, of the pedagogue and doctrinal anarchist Francisco Ferrer proved a tactical error, if not too a miscarriage of justice, which stirred liberal and socialist opinion throughout Europe. Maura, the conservative leader, was forced out of office after two and a half years, the first tenure of any length that the reign had seen, and there long persisted a violent antagonism to conservative rule.

This "tragic week," though instigated by anarcho-syndicalists and unrelated to Catalanism, added a further count in the developing tension between Catalonia and Madrid. Since the elections of 1901 Catalan "regionalists" had had representation as such in both houses of parliament, their aim "to work by all legitimate means for the autonomy of the Catalan people within the Spanish state." The cause received strong impetus from the passing in 1906 of a notorious "law of jurisdictions," one provision of which enacted the long-standing army demand that activities directed against the armed forces should be tried by military tribunals. This frankly political weapon aimed directly at Catalonia became the most hated, as it was the most illiberal, measure of the whole twenty-five years during which it remained in force.

Among its results was the formation of a united front on the regionalist issue, the Solidaritat Catalana, which though soon sundered contributed to the winning of a first notable concession from Madrid, the creation in 1914 of a "Mancomunitat" or federation of the four Catalan provinces invested with certain powers and functions — notably communications, education, and social services — hitherto reserved to the central government. A modest instalment of the full autonomy demanded, and far from settling the "Catalan problem," it marked a reversal of that policy of centralization which the Habsburgs had begun and Philip V so ruthlessly completed, and it allowed the Catalans to demonstrate once again the capacity for running their own affairs which had always been the envy and despair of the Castilian.

In one direction Canalejas and the liberals sought to march with the times. The Church's monopoly control of education in a country where half the children received no schooling and its intolerance of religious dissent continued to irk the more enlightened sectors of public opinion; while the religious orders, greatly swollen after the expulsions from France of 1905, had come under heavy criticism as parasitical.

In 1910 Canalejas proposed to the Vatican revision of the 1851 concordat, required the civil registration of orders, and forbade the establishment meantime of new religious houses. An outburst of anti-clerical agitation led to another period of strained relations with the Vatican, but again this proved too strong for the reformers.

The World War of 1914–18 found Spain deeply divided. Army, Church, and conservatives generally inclined to Germany, who dangled the old baits of Gibraltar and a free hand with Portugal. Liberalism had with it in supporting the allies the bulk of popular opinion, together with the Basque and Catalan regionalists, who knew well on which side their interests lay. Neutrality was thus the only possible policy, and the war years witnessed in consequence a rapid industrial expansion, with corresponding strains in the social fabric. Among these must be numbered the now large-scale influx into Barcelona of unskilled labour from Murcia and Almería. In 1917 labour unrest on the railways developed into a general strike with revolutionary ends in view. It had the support, exceptionally, of both socialist and anarcho-syndicalist unions, normally engaged in bitter strife against each other, and for three months the country was under martial law.

Much more sinister was the emergence in the previous year of army "defence juntas," the equivalent of a military trade union. Behind the direct challenge these implied to government authority some suspected the hand of the king himself, who in his personal relations with the armed forces had from the beginning laid himself open to the charge of unconstitutionalism. The defence juntas marked the beginning of the end. So supported, the army won every time it saw or imagined it saw its interests invaded, and normal government became impossible. The year 1917 witnessed four governments and a long succession of crises; a cabinet in 1918 of all the talents composed of ex-premiers fared no better.

The end of the war found the country a prey therefore to both social and political unrest. Early in 1919 a threat issued in Barcelona that any "strike aggression" would be dealt with by military courts was accepted as a direct challenge and led to yet another general strike, which this time labour won, bringing down the government. Anarcho-syndicalism with its creed of violence that respected neither authority, property, nor life constituted an even graver threat to society, for which no government had the answer. In 1921 a prime minister was assassinated, in 1923 an archbishop. Catalan autonomists, confronted with this increasing lawlessness in their midst, had thus strong reason for renewing their claim to responsibilities which Madrid manifestly could not discharge. They had already, in November 1919, made petition to Madrid for full autonomy, with the support of ninety-eight per cent of all municipal and rural councils throughout the four provinces; and on rejection had gone to Versailles to invoke its concern for the rights of small nationalities and to ask for recognition in this category.

The dividing line between autonomy and separatism was crossed in 1922 by the launching of an out-and-out nationalist party, *Estat Català* [Catalan State], and for many the die had been cast: only within a federal Spain could they still want to be Spaniards. To this right wing of the movement there soon corresponded a vigorous left wing, *Acció Catalana* [Catalan Action], which in 1923 concluded an alliance with similar forces in the Basque provinces and Galicia. Once more the fate of Spain as a unitary concept was called in question: if it should collapse, warrant abounded for the contention that it would prove to be not the regions but Castile, its original maker, who now unmade it.

From Morocco in 1921 derived one more crisis, the most damaging of all. Ever since the events of 1909 the task of pacifying the protectorate and civilizing the Rif tribes had been making slow if unspectacular progress, geographical conditions being infinitely more adverse, and economic rewards less, than in the French zone. A general uprising now under Abd el Krim took the Spanish forces by surprise, and the disaster of Anual in July, when the tribesmen destroyed a force 20,000 strong and all but pushed the Spaniards into the sea at Melilla, staggered the nation. This was the army that at home was presuming to set itself above the state; and this, to many, was the crowning result of Alfonso's constant meddling, over the heads of his ministers, in spheres that were not his to invade.

There was an immediate demand, in and outside the Cortes, for a probe into responsibilities that would spare neither feelings nor reputations. The result of the enquiry was awaited, with burning national interest, in the autumn of 1923. On 13 September of that year Primo de Rivera, captain-general of Barcelona and a nephew of the namesake who as captain-general of Madrid had in 1874 proclaimed the restoration, made his *coup d'état*, disbanded government and Cortes, and, with the king's support, replaced the parliamentary farce by a military dictatorship. No more was heard of the Anual report.

The new régime enjoyed a large measure of initial goodwill, inasmuch as civilian government had manifestly broken down and the country at large was less immediately interested in the causes therefor than in the reimposition of public order. This was true even of Catalonia, until the veil was torn from the dictator's first glib professions of benevolence towards Catalan aspirations. The things a dictatorship can do well Primo de Rivera did: public security, public works, and much that lack of authority and of continuity had repeatedly frustrated before. Through joint operations with France, made possible when Abd el Krim imprudently advanced into the French zone, he rescued the army in Morocco from contumely. The Rif leader surrendered in 1926, and the reoccupation and final pacification of the whole zone followed. This in its turn lifted a crushing burden from the treasury; and in the following year, for the first time in two decades, the budget was balanced without recourse to a loan.

Political problems were less amenable to solution. The dictator, having set out to free the country from party politics, merely drove the parties underground. Catalonia he antagonized completely by the obdurate centralism of a policy that culminated in 1925 in the abolition of the Mancomunitat. The change in that year from a military "directorate" to a partly civilian cabinet, the formation of a "Patriotic Union" in 1926 and of a National Assembly or pseudo-Cortes in 1927, failed completely to win the popular support he grew increasingly conscious of needing or to compensate for the suspension of constitutional guarantees, press censorship, and government by decree; while by his clericalist policy in education he ranged the intellectuals and the universities solidly against him. The university of Madrid he closed on one occasion for eighteen months. As always, it had proved easier to liquidate an old system than to create a new. When the repercussions of the world economic crisis of 1929 reached Spain he lost the support of the army too; and in January 1930 he confessed to defeat and left the country, to die in Paris six weeks later.

The king was left with his problem. By failing to summon new Cortes within three months he too, like Charles earlier in Portugal, had broken his coronation oath; and for that crime, to a nation concerned now only to find its way back to constitutional paths, there could be no condonation, not even the defence that in so doing he had thought to serve the higher interests of the country. A first stop-gap administration under a general, a second under an admiral, meant only that politicians concerned whether with principle or with reputation refused to serve under a perjured monarch; and persecution and imprisonment were impotent to stifle their views.

When elections could no longer be denied, it was the municipal elections of April 1931, the first opportunity for a free expression of opinion in eight years, which decided the issue. Over the country as a whole the returns alleged a monarchist majority; in the large cities the republican vote was overwhelming. Alfonso accepted their verdict and followed his late dictator into exile, though without abdicating the throne, to die in Rome ten years later.

The long chain of causation begun at Anual had brought Spain back to another 1868, with the difference that a search for another occupant of the throne did not now arise. Not only the king stood discredited, but kingship too; and there was no one in 1931 to argue that this had followed on and could be held the direct result of the total discrediting first of representative government. That conviction would gain ground with the experience of the years immediately ahead. Meantime the second republic came overnight.

Primo de Rivera, in a political testament written in Paris, had observed that, whatever his failures, one undeniable success he could claim: the Catalan question would raise its head no more. Within six months, in a pact signed at San Sebastian in August 1930 by the various anti-monarchist forces, the new republic had laid its plans on the basis of full recognition for the principle of self-determination. This, to some at least of the signatories, meant clearly a federal constitution on which not Catalans alone but Basques, Galicians, and any other region so minded would have claims, a forthright reversal of the unitary trend which had presided over close on 500 years of Spanish history.

When the monarchy fell, Catalonia in its enthusiasm kept momentarily ahead of events with the proclamation, even before the republic had been hailed in Madrid, of a Catalan state "which we shall endeavour to incorporate in a federation of Iberian republics." For "state" an anxious Madrid, emphasizing that regional autonomy and a federation of republics were two very different things, secured the substi-

tution of the historic and less provocative term "Generalitat." [1] A first and profound rift had appeared before the new regime was a day old: its development would further underline fundamental realities in Spanish history which no mere change of régime can obscure. Castile is, of its essence, centralist and in consequence authoritarian. The peripheral regions are, of their essence, centrifugal and egalitarian.

Another immediate problem was public order. Dictatorship and the mailed fist had put down terrorist outrage. Their removal brought it back; and a wave of anti-clerical violence, with much burning of churches, followed by another of syndicalist strikes, spread over the country, which authority was powerless to check. It was to prove the tragedy of the republic that from the beginning its gravest dangers came precisely from the republican ranks; and before the constituent Cortes could frame its new constitution it had to pass, and later to incorporate in the same, a "law for the defence of the republic" vesting in the government and in provincial governors powers over the press, the right of association, and the individual as arbitrary and illiberal as any invoked by the dictatorship, only, as it proved, much less effective.

By the constitution of 1931 Spain was declared a "democratic republic of workers of all classes," with authority derived from the people and without official religion. It instituted a single-chamber Cortes, and gave suffrage to both sexes at the age of twenty-three. The Church was disestablished, the religious orders forbidden to teach or engage in trade, and the Society of Jesus once more deprived of its property and expelled. Divorce by consent was recognized, and primary education made compulsory. As for regionalism, groups of provinces might seek from the Cortes a statute of autonomy, but no federation of autonomous regions would be tolerated.

Regionalism apart, it was the charter of

[1] The "Generalitat" was the parliament of the independent kingdom of Aragon-Catalonia in the Middle Ages. [Editor's note.]

1812 over again, in a twentieth- instead of a nineteenth-century setting, and charged not merely with inherent contradictions, like the coupling of the ban on the teaching orders with the declaration of compulsory education while the state still provided at most for some twenty-five per cent of the school-age population, but with direct threats to the continued existence of the republic itself. One such was the giving of votes to women — more than half of the 1933 register — of whom the vast majority might be relied on to use them as their Catholic conscience, if not the priest, dictated.

The anti-clerical clauses in particular were thus political dynamite. Their formulation caused the first prime minister himself, Alcalá Zamora, and his minister of the interior to resign in protest. Azaña, succeeding as premier, might assert that Spain was no longer a Catholic nation: such wishful thinking in face of all the evidence was at one with the old presumption, never more dangerously exemplified than now, that a constitution need only reflect the society aimed at, and that the competence and the will of society as it existed to make it work could be taken for granted.

The charter safely on the statute-book, government and Cortes proceeded with the social revolution. The objectives were clear: to take the army and the Church out of politics, to break up the *latifundios* [large landed estates] and give the land to a starving peasantry, to make all men economically free and politically equal, to educate the nation, beginning with the children, into civic responsibility on a wholly secular basis, in short to make a modern society overnight out of one which was still in many respects medieval. For two years the Cortes legislated, against a background of syndicalist and communist attempts on the left to disrupt the state and of conservative, Catholic, and monarchist attempts on the right to defend the interests at the cost of which the revolution was to be effected.

The right too had been quick to show its readiness to resort to force, as in the abortive monarchist rising in Madrid and that of the army in Seville in 1932. Azaña, who had retained the ministry of war after his elevation to the premiership, had already ranged the army effectively against the republic by abolishing alike the notorious law of jurisdictions, the supreme military court, and the captaincies-general [2] of the eight military regions, by retiring — on full pay — many superfluous senior officers, and by a serious attempt to overhaul and make efficient what was much less a fighting force than a political organization.

An agrarian law, also of 1932, proposed the expropriation of large estates against indemnification and the leasing of them to the peasants in small holdings. It was centuries overdue and, had it been carried into effect, would have changed the social face of Spain: but for that twenty or thirty years, and not the five the republic lasted, were needed. The Catalan autonomy statute passed in the same year had been greatly changed and weakened in Cortes from the draft approved by the Catalans in an almost unanimous referendum. Catalonia accepted it loyally, but the disillusion went deep, and was readily fanned by later events into resentment. The corresponding Basque statute, likewise submitted in 1932, was not approved until October 1936, after the outbreak of the Civil War, and therefore never achieved reality. Still less did that for Galicia, where autonomous sentiment and the prospect of its successful implementing had alike lagged far behind.

The elections of November 1933 produced the violent swing to the right which, even without the many other factors tending in that direction, female suffrage alone would have made inevitable. Where the Cortes of 1931 had been predominantly

[2] Under the monarchy the Captain-General had been the supreme civil as well as military authority in the regional government. The abolition of the office was intended to bolster civilian supremacy at all levels of government. [Editor's note.]

left-wing, the right now numbered 207, the centre 167, and the left only 99. There followed another two years, therefore, in which policy was centre-right, with the right chafing for full power and undoing as much as it could of the work of the preceding biennium. Discontent was soon rife in Catalonia and among the Basques over the treatment they were receiving from Madrid, as in Andalusia over the dimmed outlook for agrarian reform.

A cabinet reshuffle towards the right in October 1934 loosed the avalanche with a general strike throughout the country, the proclaiming anew in Barcelona of the Catalan state within a federal republic, and in Asturias a rebellion that became a minor civil war. The revolt in Catalonia was speedily quelled by the army, now with the government and always instinctively against regionalism. That in Asturias, broken within a week with the help of Moroccan troops, left a trail of 1,335 killed, 3,000 wounded, and the city of Oviedo largely in ruins. For two months the country was under martial law. The Catalan statute was declared in abeyance, and administration again centred in Madrid. Over the question of the death penalty for rebellion the government fell, and there ensued a long period of political instability and general stultification. By the end of 1935 there had been twenty-eight governments in less than five years; and although there was now much talk and evident need of revision of the constitution, against such impermanence in office this could never be undertaken.

New elections in February 1936 ended all hope of a republic for all Spaniards, or even for all republicans. They had become a battle for power between right and left coalitions more deeply hostile to each other than ever extremes had been under the monarchy. Whichever side won, the victim would be not merely the other, but the liberal republic, and Spain. The one brought together, in a Popular Front, a strange assembly of bedfellows: republicans, socialists, syndicalists, anarchists, communists. The other boasted at least much greater cohesion in composition and coherence in programme. Between the two the centre parties were all but eliminated. In this clear-cut issue where those who had everything to lose confronted those who had nothing, there was no longer room for a middle-of-the-road policy.

More formally stated, the conflict lay between order and "progress," the two apparent incompatibles of modern Spain. The right polled slightly under or slightly over half the total votes, according to the interpretation given to marginal groupings in an election contested by close on a score of parties. The electoral system gave to the left an absolute majority of seats; and behind the façade of government its extremist elements, already wedded as all knew to direct action, set about the disintegration of the bourgeois society that was their real enemy. During the next five months there befell such a relapse into violence and chaos as had not been seen since the cantonalism[3] of 1873. Church-burnings, strikes, and political assassination paralysed the life of the country. The record for the first four months of Popular Front rule, as presented to the Cortes, was 269 murders, 170 churches, 69 political clubs, and 10 newspaper offices set on fire, and 113 general and 228 partial strikes.

And again the violence was not all on one side. Extremism on the right had begun to retaliate in kind, its instrument the Falange Española, a Spanish brand of fascism founded in 1933 by a son of the late dictator Primo de Rivera. In the south peasants were taking the agrarian law into their own hands and parcelling out the estates. The government had lost control, and the republic was already dead before it received the *coup de grâce* with the military rising launched from Morocco on 17 July 1936. Here was proof of its failure to destroy the political power of the army, as

[3] Cantonalism, named for the Swiss system of cantons, was a movement demanding that full political sovereignty be vested in the provinces and main cities of Spain rather than in the central government. [Editor's note.]

it had failed in education, in agriculture, and — with only one regular budget in its whole course — in finance. Least of all had it succeeded in inculcating the qualities of tolerance, compromise, and integrity without which there could be no self-government. And now the pronunciamiento had returned.

The Civil War of 1936–9 was fought with all the savagery and bitterness of which civil war is capable. It cost 1,000,000 lives and wrought incalculable destruction. Symbolizing in theory — for the reality was infinitely more complex — the clash between the democratic and the totalitarian way of life which was then profoundly exercising the whole of Europe, it threatened to bring all Europe into the fray. Russia poured in help to the left, Italy and Germany to the right, while England and France fought a tense and losing battle to secure from the powers more than lip-service to the principle of non-intervention. The republicans were at heavy initial disadvantage in having to build up a people's army from nothing; but the issue was not the people against the army. The nation itself was almost equally divided. . . .

The Background of the Agrarian and Clerical Problems

GERALD BRENAN

Gerald Brenan is an Englishman who made his home in an Andalusian village for the better part of fifteen years preceding the outbreak of the Civil War. *The Spanish Labyrinth*, generally accepted as the most important book written thus far concerning the background of the Civil War, combines Brenan's intimate knowledge of Spanish rural life with wide reading in Spanish history and literature. In the first of the following selections he deals with the deplorable social and economic conditions prevailing in Andalusia in the decades before 1936. In order to place Brenan's material in proper perspective the reader should note his sympathy for the anarchist outlook of the peasants among whom he lived, and his belief that the solution of Spain's agricultural problems might well involve some form of non-Soviet collectivism. To appreciate his reporting of rural wage levels, bear in mind that the peseta was worth between 10 and 15 cents during the years of which he speaks. The reader will want to ask himself what were the practical results for the rural population of the very inefficient use of land in Andalusia, and how it came about that anarchist peasants regularly voted for Catholic-Conservative candidates.

The second selection summarizes the grievances of liberals and industrial workers against the Church. It raises the following questions: Why was the Church growing in wealth and power during the years 1874–1931? What were the reasons for the struggle between the liberals and the Church regarding education? Are the complaints directed at the Christian religion or at the Church as an institutional power? Finally, does Brenan's analysis of both problems support or contradict Atkinson's interpretation?

THE INHABITANTS of Andalusia are not scattered in farms or villages (there are very few villages in the Guadalquivir Basin and the occasional farms one sees are new), but are concentrated in towns that have a population of from 8000 to 25,000. In between these towns, which generally occupy ancient Iberian sites and lie at some distance from one another, there is open country. An English or French town that has 12,000 inhabitants is a busy place. Not so an Andalusian pueblo of the same size. Let us take, for example, Osuna in the province of Seville with a population of 16,000 or else Morón with 19,000 or even Carmona with 22,000. The first impression is one of decay and stagnation. A few wretched shops selling only the bare necessities of life: one or two petty industries — soap-making, weaving of esparto mats, potteries, oil-distilleries that between them employ some couple of hundred men: the ancestral houses of the absentee landowners, dilapidated and falling into ruin: then a few bourgeois families — the overseers of the large estates or the farmers who rent from them — and who only remain here because their interests compel them to: from eight to twelve hundred families, mostly poor, who own or rent a small property or have some settled employment. And then the landless proletariat. Three-quarters of the population consists in these men and their families, who are hired by

From Gerald Brenan, *The Spanish Labyrinth* (New York, 1950), pp. 118–122, 47–55. Reprinted by permission of the Cambridge University Press.

9

the day, by the month, by the season — rarely for longer than that — by the overseers of the large estates or by the tenant farmers who rent from them. For more than half the year they are unemployed.

The more closely one examines the conditions in this area of large estates, the more terrible and shocking they are seen to be. Till the European War the landlords generally worked their estates directly under overseers. They cultivated only the best land and left the rest untilled. Starving labourers who attempted to plough it were beaten by the police. During the war it paid them to cultivate the whole of it, but since 1918 the area of uncultivated land began inevitably to grow again. In 1931, for example, there were 33,000 acres uncultivated at Osuna and 50,000 at Utrera: at Jerez de los Caballeros a certain duke kept 56,000 acres uncultivated as a shooting estate. No doubt a considerable proportion of this land was only fit for rough pasture. However, near Seville there are still 75,000 acres of the very best land given up to bull breeding, and in the province of Cadiz, where there is good rainfall, the amount of arable land employed in horse and cattle breeding is enormous.

Such a lack of self-interest in rich landowners living in Madrid or Seville may appear extraordinary, but the average aristocrat simply took the advice of his steward and did not bother his head about estates where he knew no one by sight and which he regarded very much as if they were in some distant colony. When for example the Duke of Alba, who has not got the reputation of being a bad landlord, visited his ancestral acres he did so with an equipment of lorries and tents, as though he were travelling in the centre of Africa. Very often, too, the owner did not have the capital to develop the land, and the banks would not lend it to him. And then, as Señor Madariaga has pointed out, there were sometimes special reasons for reducing the area under cultivation. By taking advantage of the unemployment so caused he could knock something off the wages

and so "reduce the rebellious workers to submission."

Since the slump that followed the war and especially since the coming of the Dictatorship the tendency of the large landowners has been to rent out more and more of their estates. In 1930 between 70 and 80 per cent of the large Andalusian estates were rented in farms of from 100 to 1000 acres. The rents paid were high — at Carmona, a typical Sevillian district, they were 6½ per cent on the capital value of the land. And it must be remembered that the landlord had no obligations — he neither paid taxes, nor kept his houses in repair nor spent money on improving his estate. E. H. G. Dobby describes how he once pointed out to a large tenant farmer the encroaching palmetto scrub on his fields. "Let the landlord see to it," was his angry reply. And so the condition of the land was slowly deteriorating. The position since 1928 of these tenant farmers, caught between a falling market and a rising wages bill, has been intolerable.

We can now approach the question of the *braceros* or landless labourers, who make up three-quarters of the population. Their wages to begin with: in 1930 they were earning on an average from 3 to 3.50 pesetas (i.e. 1s. 6d. to 1s. 9d.) for an eight-hour day during four or five months of the year. In summer — under the terrible heat of the Andalusian sun — they earned from 4 to 6 pesetas (2s. to 3s.) — for a twelve-hour day during two or three months. During the rest of the year — that is during four, five, or six months — they were unemployed. Since there were no small holdings for them to work in, no allotments, not even a patch of garden to their houses and absolutely no system of municipal or Church or State relief, they would have starved during their spells of unemployment, but for the credit given by the shops. As it was they lived in a state of chronic hunger and the deaths from malnutrition, which reach a high figure in almost every part of the Peninsula, were here particularly numerous. One cannot, even in Spain, bring up a family on from 600 to 1000 pesetas (£15 to £25) a year, without the resources that the English country-side gives of a garden or allotment, wiring a rabbit, doing an odd job here and there.

And I have not given the lowest figures. On the distant farms and in the mountain hamlets wages dropped to 2.25 pesetas a day for men and to from 1.0 to 1.25 pesetas for women. In out-of-the-way places the eight-hour day was not observed. The periods of unemployment were often even longer than five or six months, especially when there were spells of wet weather or drought, and any men whom the landlords had a grudge against failed to get work at all except during harvest. In 1930 there were over 200,000 labourers unemployed in Andalusia during the greater part of the year and after 1930 this figure increased rapidly.

During the ploughing and the harvest, which occupied several months, the labourers would leave their families and sleep at the large *cortijos,* which would often be some ten or twenty miles away from the village. They slept, men and women together, sometimes a hundred at a time, on the floor of a long room called the *gañanía,* which had a fireplace at one end. The landowner fed them: except at harvest time, when they were given beans, the only dish was *gazpacho,* a soup of oil, vinegar and water with bread floating on the top. They took it hot for breakfast, cold for lunch, hot again at night. Sometimes to this diet of maize bread and oil, potatoes and garlic would be added. When the landlord provided the food, the wages were rarely more than 1.5 pesetas, for which they generally worked 12 hours, with rests. These conditions, first described in 1904 by Blasco Ibáñez in his novel *La Bodega* and, later, by A. Marvaud and other investigators, had not appreciably changed by 1930 in Lower Andalusia, as I can testify from personal experience.

And the housing conditions: great numbers of these families did not own any furniture except a cooking pot and ate their meals like animals on the ground. But I will quote E. H. G. Dobby, whose impartiality is evident to anyone who has read his monographs.

I recall an incident during a visit (in 1935) to an experimental pig farm in an out-of-the-way part of Andalusia. From the darkness at one end of the building came a red glow. I went along and found a labourer's family crouched on the floor round a twig fire with smoke so thick that breathing was difficult. The malodorous squalor contrasted with the carefully washed sties that I had been seeing. To my query an old woman mumbled: "Yes, we live here. Worse than the pigs." At which the owner beside me exclaimed indignantly: "You have a roof over your head. What more do you want?"

Such wages, such conditions to-day may seem almost incredible. They are unique in Europe. And yet the tenant farmers, under the pressure of high rents and taxes and falling markets, cannot afford to pay more. For since 1850, and indeed from far earlier times, there has been a steady competition between landowner and labourer, the first to see how little he can pay, and the latter to see how little he can work. Andalusian workmen, given the opportunity, are the hardest working and most skilled manual labourers in Spain. After all they are many of them the descendants of the "industrious Moors" of the history books, few of whom ever came from Morocco. But when so many of their comrades are unemployed, it becomes a point of honour with them to do as little work as possible. And they are also well aware of the manner in which they are exploited. In these towns the atmosphere of hatred between classes — of tenant for landlord, of landless proletariat for everyone who employs him — has to be seen to be believed. Since the Republic came in many landlords have been afraid to visit their estates. And the labourers are all Anarchists. What else can one expect under such conditions — miserable pay, idleness for half the year and semi-starvation for all of it? The herding together of labourers for months at a time away from their families also increases their receptivity to revolutionary ideas. And legal methods of protesting are ruled out: the cacique system is at its worst in Andalusia and regularly at every election Catholic-Conservative deputies are returned for Anarchist constituencies. When force ceases to be possible, bribery takes its place, and down to the last election of 1936 tens of thousands of starving labourers took the money or promises of work of the landlords and voted for their candidates.

*   *   *

From 1874, then, to 1931 the Church, though losing every year its influence with the poor, was gaining steadily in riches and in political power. The death of Alfonso XII led to a great strengthening of its position. In return for Leo XIII's special protection (which kept off the danger of a Carlist rising during the King's minority) the Queen Regent dealt out money and patronage with a lavish hand. Indeed as she was herself entirely under the influence of her confessor she scarcely needed this encouragement. At the same time the French regular clergy, who had been compelled to leave their homes by the Jules Ferry laws secularizing education, established themselves in Spain and a concerted effort began to save at least one country in Europe from "liberal atheism." Within a few years the Peninsula was studded with almost as many convents, colleges and religious foundations as it had seen during its palmiest period and the court, the universities, the press and indeed a large part of the governing classes went down before a wave of clericalism.

The leaders of this movement were, of course, the Jesuits. Theirs was the policy — originated three centuries before by their founder — of winning over the rich and the powerful. For this they needed money. And indeed Spain provided a tempting

investment for the general funds of their Society: money laid out there would bring not only a good return but also immediate political power. And so their wealth in the Peninsula began to mount up — composed as it was of the investments of the Society abroad and of the new bequests made by the pious in Spain — until it reached really immense proportions. In 1912, according to Joaquín Aguilera, Secretary of the Fomento,[1] they controlled "without exaggeration one-third of the capital wealth of Spain." They owned railways, mines, factories, banks, shipping companies, orange plantations. There came to be something almost mythical about their industrial activities. One was told that they ran the antique furniture business, supplied Madrid with fresh fish and controlled the liveliest of the cabarets. Their working capital was said to amount to £60,000,000 sterling. There is of course no reason why the Jesuits, with their colleges and missions to provide for, should not be wealthy. They would not be able to carry out their work if they were not. And there is a Spanish saying: *El dinero es muy católico*: "Money is a good Catholic." But it seemed scarcely in the national interests that one section of the community — and that a militant one — should control so large a share of the industrial life of the country, and then one must remember that a good part of this wealth had to be acquired by cadging for gifts and bequests among the rich and that these favours were not given for nothing. In return the Church was expected to defend the interests of the rich against the poor. How close, how intimate, how unbecoming this connection between some of the religious orders and the very rich could be is scarcely to be credited by those who have not lived for some years in Spain. For more than a century now all contact with the rich, with the court, and with politics in Spain has been corrupting.

[1] A businessmen's society for the promotion of industrial development in the Barcelona area. [Editor's note.]

On the other hand the country clergy were poor. Their salaries, fixed by the Concordat of 1851, were paid by the State and the cost of living had been rising. Some of them scarcely received more than a manual labourer. But poverty is never humiliating in Spain. On the contrary, it is apt to bring out the best in the Spanish character, so that thought badly educated and somewhat lax by modern standards (there were many who still adhered to the mediaeval custom of *barraganía* and kept a "housekeeper") [2] they were usually plain, honest men, who in an age when faith was dead did their best to carry out their duties.

There were then the monastic orders. By the provisions of the Concordat only three orders were allowed in Spain — two of which were specified and one which was left to the Pope to choose. He never chose and so every order that wished to established itself. On various occasions the Liberals attempted to regulate this position — to compel them at least to register and so submit to inspection, but each time such furious protests were raised, there were so many threats from Rome and from the Archbishops, that the attempt had to be dropped. Actually the number of monks was never very great — some 10,000 when the Republic came in, most of them schoolmasters — but the number of nuns rose to be 40,000, more than had ever been known in Spain before and at least twice as many as in the time of St. Theresa.

But the main struggle with the Liberals was over education. Until 1836 education had been almost entirely in the hands of the higher clergy and the religious orders. The Church at this time had not yet re-

[2] In the Middle Ages it was an established custom, permitted by the bishops, for Spanish priests to have concubines. They wore a special dress and had special rights and were called *barraganas*. When the Council of Trent forbade this practice to continue, the Spanish clergy protested. And in fact they have never paid much attention to the prohibition, for they continue to have "housekeepers" and "nieces" to this day. Their parishioners, far from being shocked, prefer them to live in concubinage, as otherwise they would not always care to let their womenfolk confess to them. [Author's note.]

covered from the shock which the French Revolution had given it and had a mortal dread of learning. Science, mathematics, agriculture and political economy were therefore not taught, as they were considered dangerous subjects for any but trained theologians. The Jesuits frowned on history, which offered so many bad examples to the young and innocent. Almost the only subject that could usefully be studied at the universities was law. For though medicine was taught, it suffered from the suppression of that erroneous Lutheran notion upon the circulation of the blood, whilst if one touched on physics one had to remember that the Copernican system was still a *cosa de Inquisición*. In the elementary schools the children of the poor were deliberately not taught to read, but only to sew and to recite the Catechism. As the University of Cervera — the only university in Catalonia — declared in its famous address to Ferdinand VII: "Far be from us the dangerous novelty of thinking."

The Liberal Revolution changed this. Successive Governments gradually freed the universities from clerical control and laid the foundations of universal elementary education. The religious orders then turned their attention to secondary schools. The Church set itself the task of educating all the sons of the upper and upper-middle classes. The colleges of the Jesuits and Augustinians became what the public schools are in England. One cannot altogether say that it was a good education that they gave. "The Jesuits do not educate, they domesticate," wrote the Conde de la Mortera, whilst those who did not take the imprint preserved bitter memories of the corporal punishments and of the system of sneaking and espionage which prevailed in their colleges. Some of the most intransigent of the anti-clericals owed their hatred of the Church to these early impressions. Nor was the purely scholastic side of the education they gave what might have been expected. The humanities (Latin, history and literature) were all

badly taught and so was religion, but there
was a high standard on technological subjects. The Jesuits, for example, had two
universities that gave degrees in law and
commerce and a large and efficient institute for engineers and electricians. The
most important technical electrical maga-
zine in the country was run by them. On
this territory the Government did not com-
pete. The *Institución Libre de Enseñanza,*
one of the best and most famous educational establishments in Europe, which has
done more to raise the level of Spanish culture than any other single institution, was
founded in 1876 by private enterprise.

But it was over primary education that
the main battle took place. The field was
a wide one, for in 1870 something like 60
per cent of the population was illiterate.
Though the majority of existing schools
belonged to the civil authorities (the policy of the religious orders in the early nineteenth century had been to prevent the
poor from learning to read) both sides
claimed a monopoly. The tactics of the
Church were to force the State schools to
close down from lack of funds. As the
upkeep of the schools was then a charge
on the municipalities, by its influence on
the caciques and local administrations the
Church was able to prevent any payments
from being made. It was then that the saying "to be as hungry as a schoolmaster"
first came into existence. In a country
where more than two-thirds of the population are permanently under-nourished, it
conveys a good deal. This state of affairs
was only remedied in 1901 when Ro-
manones made education a charge on the
State, but the amount devoted to it on the
budget was still scandalously small.

To appreciate the full intransigeance of
the attitude of the Church one must remember that at all events down to 1910
the immense majority of schoolmasters
were sincere Catholics and went to mass
regularly: that the Catholic religion and
catechism were compulsorily taught in all
the schools and that the parish priest had

a right to supervise this. So far did this
sometimes go that parents used to com-
plain that in State schools the children
passed half their class hours in saying the
rosary and in absorbing sacred history and
never learned to read. The difference between a convent school and a State school
was not one of religion but of politics. To
put it bluntly, the children in convent
schools were taught that if they associated
with Liberals, they went to hell. This attitude is expressed very clearly in the complete Church catechism, republished in
1927.

"What does Liberalism teach?" it begins.
"That the State is independent of the
Church." And it goes on to point out that
the State must be subject to the Church as
the body to the soul, as the temporal to the
eternal. It then enumerates, among the
false liberties of Liberalism, liberty of conscience, of education, of propaganda and
of meeting — all of which it is heretical to
believe in. It continues:

"What kind of sin is Liberalism?" — "It
is a most grievous sin against faith."

"Why?" — "Because it consists in a collection of heresies condemned by the
Church."

"Is it a sin for a Catholic to read a Liberal newspaper?" He may read the Stock
Exchange News.

"What sin is committed by him who
votes for a Liberal candidate?" — "Generally a mortal sin."

When one remembers how timid, respectable and conservative was the Liberal
party of those days, how the very most
they demanded were those liberties current
in all other civilized countries of the world,
one sees how difficult it was not to be
thrown into an attitude of violent resistance to a party which in the last three centuries had forgotten everything and
learned nothing. The Church presented
in Spain and insoluble problem, and when
in the end the majority of the population
abandoned it in despair at its political intransigeance and burned churches and

killed priests in revolutionary — I might almost say in true Catholic and filial — anger there is surely nothing to be surprised at.

It may be argued, of course, that only by an attitude of rigid intransigeance can a religious body survive in the destructive air of the modern world. The attractive power of a Church lies to a large extent in its air of certainty, which translated into action means intolerance. But the errors of the Spanish Church have not proceeded from the depth of its conviction, but on the contrary from its lack of religious feeling combined with pride. Just as in the sixteenth century it showed neither the will nor the patience necessary for converting the Moors, but used its influence with the State to have them driven out altogether, so to-day it has refused (until too late) to take the appropriate measures for arresting the steady de-Christianization of the working classes. Disdaining the slow work of example and persuasion, it has preferred to fall back upon the authority of the State. Thus instead of meeting the Socialists and the Anarchists on their own ground, with labour organizations, friendly societies and projects for social reform, it has concentrated its efforts upon the search for a government that would suppress its enemies by force and restore to the Catholic religion the privileged position it held two centuries ago. This has meant that its action has been mainly political and, since its allies have naturally been taken from the wealthiest and most reactionary classes, that it has drawn upon itself in the course of the struggle the hostility of every decent or progressive force in the country. This hostility has done it untold harm. The educated classes have been driven to regard the Church as the enemy not only of parliamentary government but of modern European culture: the working classes have seen in it a barrier to their hopes of a better standard of living. Behind every act of public violence, every curtailment of liberty, every judicial murder, there

stood the bishop, who either in his pastoral or in a leading article of the Catholic press showed his approval and called for more. When one remembers that this political intransigeance often covered the greatest laxity of conduct and a more or less total absence of the Christian virtues, one cannot be surprised that the Church became to large sections of Spaniards the symbol of everything that was vile, stupid and hypocritical. The devotion of individual priests and monks, the sincerity and humanity which large numbers of Spanish Catholics have always shown, were obscured by the militant and reactionary attitude of the hierarchy.

Under these circumstances it is perhaps natural that, over more than two-thirds of its surface, Spain was ceasing to be a Catholic country. Already in 1910 civil marriages and funerals, almost unheard of in the previous century, were becoming common. The majority still made use of religious ceremonies at births, deaths and marriages and flocked to the great festivals, but they expressed open incredulity on Church dogmas, never attended mass and never confessed. Among the middle classes (that is to say among the men, for the women less readily lost their faith) scepticism was becoming common, and a certain contempt for the Church and clergy and for all that pertained to them had become the fashion even among those who passed as believers. By 1931 this process had reached surprising lengths. According to Father Francisco Peiró only 5 per cent of the villagers of New Castile and Central Spain attended mass or carried out their Easter obligations: in Andalusia the attendance of men was 1 per cent: in many villages the priest said mass alone. The position in Madrid was no better. In the parish of San Ramón in the quarter of Vallecas, out of a population of 80,000 parishioners, only 3½ per cent (excluding the children in the convent schools) attended mass: 25 per cent of the children born were not baptized. Of those educated in convent schools, 90 per cent did not confess or hear mass after leaving school. Yet this parish was one of the richest in Spain and spent large sums on charity and education. The situation in other parishes was worse: in that of San Millán, for example, though the church-goers were mostly drawn from the old, more than 40 per cent died without sacraments. And Barcelona and Valencia had the reputation of being more irreligious than Madrid.

A large part of this decay of religious belief was due of course simply to the spirit of the age: much the same thing was taking place in other countries. There were, however, two points that distinguished the situation in Spain from that elsewhere: first the village priests had failed (except in the north) to hold their parishioners, who had lost their faith even before Socialist or Anarchist propaganda began to reach them: then the attitude of the working classes and of the petite bourgeoisie in the towns towards the priests and monks was not one of indifference but of hatred. The reason for this was, as I have said, the militant attitude of the hierarchy in political questions; that is to say, it was a reflection of the attitude of the Church towards them and their claims. But the degree of hatred shown was often startling. If the Spanish Church is to be described as fanatical, the same word must equally be applied to many of the anti-clericals. And since fanaticism leads to credulity, on each side there grew up a firm belief in the power and wickedness of the occult forces of their adversaries: in the one case of the freemasons and supposed Russian agents and on the other of the monks and Jesuits. Of all the many antagonisms that during the last forty years have flourished in Spain, none was more bitter or envenomed than that between the Catholic Church and its opponents. The Civil War has shown to what tragic consequences it could lead.

I have said that the Church made no serious effort to keep the loyalty of the working classes by means of Catholic associations and friendly societies. This statement requires some modification. It began to take a few tentative steps in this direction in the eighties and nineties as part of the new labour policy inaugurated by Leo XIII. The Catholic associations founded then had certain initial advantages over Socialist and Anarchist trade unions: they had considerable sums of money at their disposal and by their influence over employers and landowners they could obtain a privileged position for their members. But the landlords and employers showed their usual inertia and indifference and, except at periodic moments of alarm following strikes or labour disturbances, they did not back the Catholic associations effectively. Moreover, the organizers of these associations often found themselves placed in a difficult position. They could not get sufficient members unless they could make it clear that at moments of crisis they really stood for the interests of the workmen against the employers. But this they obviously did not and could not do. The employers, who provided most of the money and guaranteed jobs to the unemployed, expected in return to use the Catholic unions to break strikes. This the workmen disliked doing. And so, at the end of years of spasmodic work and effort, the Catholic associations were forced to admit their complete failure except in certain districts in the north of Spain — Navarre, Old Castile, the Basque provinces — where the gulf between rich and poor was not so unbridgeable. Elsewhere it either happened that the Anarchists or the Socialists ousted them, or that the peasants continued without organizations of any kind. In other words the Church was so deeply compromised with the employer classes that workmen and peasants could not be lured into their associations. However, one must admit that, even if this had not been the case, the role of the Catholic leaders would not have been an easy one: given the economic situation, the wide gulf between rich and poor and the Spanish temperament, strong class antagonism was inevitable in a large part of the country. Taking sides had become necessary. And had the Church been drawn into serious support of the working classes, they would undoubtedly have seen the greater part of their present allies, the *gente de orden*,[3] leave them. . . .

[3] Literally, "persons of order." The phrase is commonly used to refer to those who refuse all reforms on the grounds that the Spaniards are so volatile that any change must involve serious disorder. [Editor's note.]

Church Burnings and the Religious Clauses
of the Constitution of 1931

E. ALLISON PEERS

The late Professor E. Allison Peers, of the University of Liverpool, was a highly respected scholar in the Castilian and Catalan literatures who counted among his friends many Spanish intellectuals of both monarchist and republican outlook. He himself was skeptical of the Republic and scornful of its anticlerical tendencies. *The Spanish Tragedy* was written in late 1936, during the Civil War which brought suffering and exile to many of his close friends. The following selections deal with various aspects of the Church crisis of 1931. The first selection describes the background of the May 11 Church burnings, the mob violence, and the helplessness of the provisional government in the face of that violence. The second describes the constitutional clauses relating to the Church, and the third passage describes the Cortes debate and the cabinet crisis of October, 1931.

The reader should consider the following questions: What was the significance of the attitude of Cardinal Segura? Why was the government unable to restore order immediately on May 11? Why should the constitutional articles concerning the rights and functions of the Church be included among the "political and individual guarantees" of all Spaniards? Why was Prime Minister Azaña so insistent that the Orders not be permitted to teach in the future? Considering the readings as a whole, do you find the author just and objective in his description of these events?

THE TROUBLES of May 1931 began with a journalistic scoop achieved by the famous Monarchist newspaper *A.B.C.* The editor of *A.B.C.*, Sr. Luca de Tena, had, like his father, its founder, long been the personal friend of Don Alfonso XIII, and, three weeks after the proclamation of the Republic, he had paid a visit to the King, who was now in London, to secure a personal interview, which became the sensation of the moment. There was nothing in the content of the interview, as we look back on it to-day, which was in the least degree inflammatory; indeed the remarkable feature of it is that the exiled King could express himself with such moderation. "I will not put the slightest difficulty in the way of the Republican Government," he was reported as saying.

Monarchists who wish to follow my adivce will not only refrain from placing obstacles

From E. Allison Peers, *The Spanish Tragedy* (London, 1937), pp. 51–59, 64–66, 70–74. Reprinted by permission of Methuen & Co., Ltd.

in the Government's path but will support it in all patriotic enterprises. . . . High above the formal ideas of republic or monarchy stands Spain. . . . I may have made mistakes but I have thought only of the good of Spain. . . . I declined the offers made me to remain and rule by force and . . . for Spain I made the greatest sacrifice of my life when I found she no longer desired me.

It was not the sentiments expressed in the interview that alarmed Republican opinion so much as the facts that the editor of a leading newspaper had travelled to London to get it; that, having got it, he had written it up so attractively and featured it with such prominence; and that he had added to it an expression of loyalty to the "Parliamentary and Constitutional Monarchy." Nor was it so much the content of Cardinal Segura's famous pastoral that incensed this opinion as the words in which the Cardinal had clothed it and the feeling that he could not be relied upon to remain neutral.

The striking and dynamic personality of Dr. Pedro Segura, Cardinal-Archbishop of Toledo and Primate of all Spain, could hardly be kept for long in the background at a time of national turmoil. A Bishop at thirty-five, Primate and Cardinal eleven years later, he was still on the right side of fifty. A scholar, he had won no less than three doctorates at college. A social reformer, he had become known throughout Spain for his humanitarian work in its most poverty-stricken region, Las Hurdes. A devoted pastor, he lived the simplest of lives in his Toledan palace, and, during diocesan missions, had been known to work as hard and as long as the humblest parish priest.

Since the fourteenth of April, report had been busy as to the attitude of the Cardinal-Archbishop to the new *régime,* and on the very day after the publication of the A.B.C. interview, the Press reproduced the long text of a pastoral which set the entire country talking. By no means the whole of it could be interpreted as provocative, but the language and the sentiments of several

paragraphs, on which the Press naturally laid emphasis, were, to say the least of it, unfortunate. It was hardly prudent, for instance, at such a time, to begin by expressing "grateful remembrance of His Majesty King Alfonso XIII, who during his reign successfully preserved the ancient traditions of faith and piety of his ancestors," to devote the three following paragraphs to a eulogy of "his fallen Majesty" and to hint that "the enemies of the kingdom of Jesus Christ" are advancing. The climax of his argument was nothing less than a call to battle.

In these moments of terrible uncertainty, every Catholic must measure the magnitude of his responsibilities and valiantly perform his duty. If we all keep our eyes fixed on higher interests, and sacrifice what is secondary to what is important; if we unite our forces and prepare to fight with perfect cohesion and discipline, without vain parade, but with faith in our ideals, with abnegation and the spirit of sacrifice, we shall be able to look at the future with tranquillity, confident of victory.

If we remain "quiet and idle"; if we allow ourselves to give way to "apathy and timidity"; if we leave the road open to those who are attempting to destroy religion or expect the benevolence of our enemies to secure the triumph of our ideals, we shall have no right to lament when bitter reality shows us that we had victory in our hands, yet knew not how to fight like intrepid warriors, prepared to succumb gloriously.

From one point of view these were splendid words; none will deny that they were brave words; yet most people to-day would agree that they were also provocative words. It was not surprising that an anti-clerical Minister of Justice should condemn them as "bellicose," or that the Government should decide that this kind of thing "could not be permitted to continue" and request the Holy See to remove the Cardinal from his archbishopric. Nor could it be wondered at that A.B.C., when it described the pastoral as "irreproachably loyal to the Government" and saw in it "not a paragraph, assertion or counsel that was open to question," should be attacked by extremists.

This, and more, was what happened. On Sunday, May 10, exactly four weeks after those momentous municipal elections which put an end to the Monarchy, Spain's immaculate republic soiled its record.

The trouble began in Madrid, where, in the Calle de Alcalá, a new Monarchist Club had been founded, and on this Sunday morning was holding a private meeting to elect its Committee. Some reports had it that passers-by heard the Royal March being played inside the house on a gramophone; others alleged that members of the Club were indulging in provocative demonstrations from the balcony. Whatever the cause, a crowd collected, and when two men paying off their taxi before entering the Club heard the commotion, cried "Long live the Monarchy!" and struck their driver, who had shouted for the Republic, its smouldering passion was kindled. A free fight began — and unfortunately it began in the pre-luncheon hour when the Alcalá is always packed to capacity.

Somehow a rumour started that the taxi-driver had died from the effect of the blows he had received. The rumour spread like wildfire.

"Down with the Monarchists!" yelled the crowds. "Down with the house! Down with the balcony!"

By this time the Civil Guard had arrived in force, but its attempt to disperse the crowds was completely ineffective. The excellent idea was circulating that it would be an amusing game to set fire to the waiting cars of the members of the Club before their own eyes. No sooner said than done: in a few minutes two of the cars were blazing merrily.

From the standpoint of the authorities, the problems of how to clear the streets and of how to get the Monarchists safely out of the house were now equally pressing. Three large police motor-vans were brought, and, to the accompaniment of jeers, curses and blows, the members of the Club were packed inside. But none of them could go, for scores of men flung themselves on the ground to impede their passage. At last the Home Secretary, Don Miguel Maura, mounted one of the vans and tried to harangue the crowd. Worse and worse! "What! Maura?" yelled the mob. "Down with him! Down with the son of his father! Down with the Monarchist's son!"

By this time it was four o'clock. The driver of one of the motor-vans, by means of a pretty reverse feint, had managed to clear a way through the human barrier which impeded his progress, but the crowds grew larger and larger, till the whole of the Alcalá and the streets beyond it were one mass of humanity.

Then suddenly some one started a new cry:

"*A.B.C.!* To the offices of *A.B.C.!* Down with *A.B.C.!*"

Instantly the situation changed. In a few moments, thousands were charging down the Alcalá, across the Cibeles square, up the Paseo de Recoletos and by all other possible routes until they joined forces in the Calle de Serrano, where the offices of the Monarchist daily were situated. On their way they recognized Don Leopoldo Matos, a former minister of King Alfonso, paying an afternoon call. Immediately they set upon him, pummelled him, beat him, tore off his coat, trampled on his hat, and might well have lynched him had he not, for his own safety, been taken into custody.

At last, after a number of such incidents, the crowd arrived at its goal. A few sentries who had been detailed to guard the offices were soon disposed of, and in a few moments, to the cheering of thousands, several hundred people were engaged in stoning the windows and flinging petrol on the walls with the intention of setting them on fire. The Civil Guard, in desperation, retreated into the building and thence fired several shots into the air. This sufficed to disperse the crowd, which, unlike similar crowds of later days, was unarmed, and soon groups of frenzied Republicans, with tales of machine-guns being trained on them from the *A.B.C.* offices, were busy working off their hostility on buildings in other parts of the city. The Government, as though completely unprepared for events which had been freely forecast, appeared to be powerless, and all the Home Secretary could do that night was to attempt to appease the mob by announcing that *A.B.C.* had been suspended, its offices searched and its editor put into prison.

But the blood of the mob was up and on the next day incendiarism, directed this time against the Church, began in earnest. In broad daylight — to be exact, at half-past ten in the morning — a body of men set fire to the Jesuit Church of the Calle de la Flor, in the very centre of the capital. Not till it was completely alight did firemen arrive, and then the crowds, who had been watching the scene as placidly as though it were a municipal firework-display, set upon them and prevented them forcibly from extinguishing the flames till the church was burned to the ground. Even mounted police and cavalry could do little against this determination of the people.

Next, crowds with red flags formed up and marched to the magnificent new convent and church built by the Carmelite Fathers in the Plaza de España, to the residence of the Jesuits in Alberto Aguilera, to the Mercedarian convent in Bravo Murillo, to the College of Maravillas in the suburb of Cuatro Caminos, to the College of the Sacred Heart in Chamartín, and to a number of other buildings, all of which they set on fire and more or less completely destroyed. Many convents were disbanded as a precaution, and monks, friars and nuns escaped in lay attire. Some of them wandered through Madrid that night, with nowhere to go, and were taken in by private families.

Still the Government failed to take effective action. The Cabinet sat continuously

for thirteen hours, but about the results of their long deliberations the less said the better. In an official statement they laid the principal blame, not, as might have been expected, upon the mobs, but upon the most unpopular people in Spain, whom any stick was good enough to beat — the Monarchists. These "reactionaries," ran the statement, had "deliberately chosen to excite disturbances" and to "defy the people." Even the circumstantial accounts of the disturbances given by the staunchest of Republican papers belied this imputation. But its effect was, of course, merely to stimulate the crowds to further effort, and the suspension of the Catholic daily *El Debate,* as well as of the Monarchist *A.B.C.*, could hardly have been more timely if its object had been to applaud the incendiaries' achievements. For the rest, martial law was proclaimed, the Exchange was closed and an appeal was made to the country by radio.

But, though the Madrid mobs had by now had their fill of violence, the fires so light-heartedly set ablaze at once spread over the country. North of Madrid there were no disturbances, nor in Catalonia, which was occupied, as we shall see, with other matters. But in Andalusia — *tierra de María Santísima; tierra bendita de Dios*[1] — a terrible toll was taken by ungoverned passion. In almost all the large cities of the South martial law was proclaimed. In Valencia, Alicante, Murcia, Granada, Seville, Córdoba, Cádiz and Málaga, convents and churches went a-blazing. The city hit worst of all was Málaga, where on May 11 and 12 fires continued uninterruptedly. Not only were the Episcopal Palace, the Jesuits' residence and convents of Augustinians, Carmelites and Marists set on fire, but various churches, containing valuable works of art, were destroyed, together with numerous shops and public buildings.

For forty-eight hours something like panic reigned in Spain and men talked

[1] "Land of the Most Holy Virgin; land blessed by God." [Editor's note.]

wildly of Russia and Mexico. There was much removal of Church treasures to places of safety. In the midst of it all, the Cardinal-Primate, not without suggestions from the secular authorities, slipped quietly over the frontier and made his way to Rome. But at the end of five days the country was completely quiet again. The wave of feeling which had surged up, without, as it seemed, any adequate cause, had subsided with equal suddenness. *A.B.C.* and the *Debate* remained suspended; a few public functionaries resigned their posts; and newspaper reporters began hunting for news again.

So ended the first calendar month of the second Spanish Republic.

The attacks on churches and convents demonstrated clearly to the Government the necessity for more effective control of mob-passion, and there is no doubt that they profited from the lesson. The strengthening of the Civil Guard, a brave and loyal body of men to whom all pay tribute, dates from this period, as does the establishment of the more drastically intentioned Shock Troops, or Guardias de Asalto. But for the moment the chief effect which the outbreaks seemed to have was the straining of relations between Church and State which even now were none too easy. Already, before it had been a week in office, the Government had announced the secularization of cemeteries, the cancellation of compulsory church parades in the Army and a more ample toleration for non-Catholic worship. At the end of May a decree was passed giving all denominations equal rights as to worship, forbidding any functionary to inquire into an individual's religious beliefs, and removing the obligations on individuals to take part in religious practices or ceremonies. Unhappily, there were those who interpreted this to mean that Catholics might be persecuted with impunity, and numbers of practising Catholics, in no way connected with politics, lost their employment for reasons (to quote a phrase which was made to cover a multitude of sins about

that time) of "Incompatibility with the *régime*."

Meanwhile, to the virtual expulsion from Spain of the Cardinal-Primate had to be added the actual expulsion of the Bishop of Vitoria, who was alleged to have used diocesan visitations for purposes of political propaganda. It seemed as if a complete impasse had been reached between Madrid and Rome when the Holy See refused its *placet* [diplomatic recognition] to the newly appointed Ambassador to the Vatican and made a condition of his being accepted the safeguarding of the lives and property of the faithful. The Government issued no reply to this announcement, for it had no reply to make. At that time it was incapable of safeguarding the lives or property of any group of citizens whatsoever.

Perhaps the tension caused by this situation of mutual inactivity was somewhat relieved by an undignified incident which occurred in the middle of June. The Cardinal-Primate made a secret return to Spain — *incognito*. Evidently, though he had not been formally expelled, he was aware that the frontier officers would not re-admit him, so this Prince of the Church re-entered Spain by one of the little-used Pyrenean passes, and it was not till he had reached Guadalajara that he was stopped, detained for the night and on the next day ejected by way of Irún. Whether because the blow was too much for his pride or because the Holy See thought it best to yield to the demands of the Spanish Government, he never repeated the attempt. Shortly afterwards, his see was declared vacant, and he was succeeded in it by Mgr. Goma, of Tarazona, an elderly man who proved to have considerable administrative ability, though at the time of his appointment he was noted chiefly for his prowess in theology.

*   *   *

THE CONSTITUTION AND THE CHURCH

Following a brief section on Spanish nationality comes the longest and in many ways the most important section of the entire document — on "political and individual guarantees." Of this the dominant notes are equality and freedom. No titles of nobility are henceforth recognized. No special privileges are to be accorded to citizens on account of sex, wealth, social class, political opinions or religious beliefs. All are free to choose their professions, and to "express in any form their ideas and opinions, without previously being subjected to censorship." Both sexes are given the franchise, on equal terms; the age for enfranchisement is fixed at twenty-three. These and other provisions clearly do their utmost to create a free Spain. At any time of national emergency, however, many of them may be "totally or partially suspended, by decree of the Government, over either the whole or a part of the country," subject to subsequent confirmation by the Cortes. The suspension can last only for a maximum period of thirty days without renewal.

This vital section of the new Constitution also contains some of the most hotly debated of its clauses — those relating to religion and the religious Orders. The payment of the clergy by the State is to come to an end after two years from the promulgation of the Constitution. No favour or financial aid is to be given to any religious institution by State, provinces or municipalities. All religious confessions are henceforth to be considered as societies, subjected to a special law. The freedom of conscience already guaranteed to the individual by decree is reassured to him; he may profess and practise any form of religion provided it does not transgress public morals. All denominations may worship as they please in private, but for any public manifestation of their religion they must obtain the sanction of the Government.

Of the religious Orders, those which require a vow to be taken, "besides the three canonical vows, of obedience to an authority other than the legitimate authority of the State," "are dissolved" and "their property is to be nationalized and used for educative and charitable purposes." All other Orders will come under the scope of a special law which will dissolve such of them as (presumably in the opinion of the Government of the day) "constitute a peril to the safety of the State" and oblige the remainder to register with the Ministry of Justice. No Order shall be permitted to hold more property, directly or indirectly, than it needs for its own subsistence. No Order shall engage in industry, commerce or education. All Orders shall be obliged to submit their annual accounts to the State and (a final threat held over the heads of the contumacious)" it shall be permissible for the property of the religious Orders to be nationalized."

Lest it should be thought that the Orders are unduly penalized, further articles proceed to declare that "all the wealth of the country, whosesoever it be, is subordinated to the interests of the national economy" and that "all the historical and artistic wealth of the country, whosesoever it be, constitutes the nation's cultural treasure and is under the safe custody of the State, which may prohibit its exportation and alienation and decree the legal expropriations which it deems opportune for its defence." In no circumstances may the confiscation of property be ordered as a penalty, but any property may be "forcibly expropriated," conditionally upon the approval of the Cortes, "on payment of an adequate indemnity." Adequacy, as we shall shortly see, is a term susceptible of varied interpretations.

Another group of articles regulates marriage, divorce, and the education of children. Marriage, in the new Spain, is to be founded on sex equality, and any union may be dissolved "as a result of mutual disagreement or on the petition of either party, just cause being shown." Parents are obliged to educate their children, legitimate or illegitimate; primary education (as previously) is to be compulsory and free; and all education will be secular and (magnificent phrase!) "inspired by ideals of human solidarity."

*   *   *

THE CRISIS OF OCTOBER 1931

The second and much more violent crisis arose from the debates on the religious question. Again and again during the history of the Second Republic the essentially religious character of the Spaniard becomes evident. Attempt after attempt is made by the enemies of religion to attack it or expel it from the minds of the people, and again and again the people themselves instinctively defend it and secure its victory. It is surely a fact of the greatest significance that at a moment of supreme enthusiasm for the Republic and at a time when its very nature was under discussion, persons of no less importance than the Prime Minister and the Home Secretary[2] should resign from the Government in defence of the Church to which they professed fidelity. It was not the first time during the debates that a secession from the Cabinet had been threatened: the Finance Minister had handed in his resignation at the end of September and the Prime Minister had done the same a week later, but in both cases pressure from the remainder of the Cabinet had kept them in their offices. Now, however, conscience dictated a course which no merely political pressure could alter, and from defeat itself the Church snatched a victory.

The anti-clerical articles described above were introduced on October 8, 1931, not by their chief supporter, Sr. Azaña, whose heavy guns were kept till the last, but by a somewhat more doctrinaire opponent of the Church, Don Fernando de los Ríos, Minister of Justice. Don Fernando had no great difficulty in making out the usual case for disestablishment: at one and the same time it increases the spiritual strength

of the Church and the financial resources of the State — an attractive argument. And although, in such discussions, disendowment is always a more delicate proposition, he made skilful work of the contention that the already poorly paid clergy might reasonably be supported by their parishes instead of by the State, which expends upon the Church an average sum of over 44,000,000 pesetas.

After a preliminary discussion on these lines, the article was sent back to a Standing Committee of the Cortes for certain revisions, and it was not until October 13, after the separation of Church and State had been agreed to, that the article on the religious Orders, which caused the split in the Cabinet, again came up for discussion. The outstanding speech in this debate, and one of the outstanding speeches in the entire history of the Second Republic, was delivered by that doughty enemy of the Orders, Sr. Azaña.

Some of the most amazing statements that have ever been made in the Cortes can be read in the Spanish equivalent of *Hansard* for October 13. First, Sr. Azaña made a pure debating point, which could hardly have influenced a single deputy: this was not a religious problem, he said, that was being discussed, but a wholly political one, since a religious problem is concerned only with the conscience of an individual and this question related to the constitution of a secular State. Then he went on, with perfect seriousness, to declare that Spain was no longer a Catholic nation! He admitted that there were still millions of practising Catholics in the country but considered that "since the last century Catholicism has ceased to be the expression and the guide of Spanish thought."

Spain in the sixteenth century was a Catholic country despite the fact that numerous and most distinguished Spaniards were dissenters, a few of whom are the glory and splendour of Spanish literature. To-day Spain has ceased to be Catholic, despite the fact that there are many millions of Spaniards who are practising Catholics.

---

[2] The Home Secretary, or Minister of the Interior, was formally responsible for public order and police actions throughout the country. The post has always been a very important and delicate one in Spanish governments under any political system. [Editor's note.]

After emitting this puny paradox, Sr. Azaña entered the realms of finance and then went on to what he described as the "dramatic" part of the Government's proposals — the treatment of the religious Orders. Here he was frank enough to show the weakness of his case side by side with its strength. It is necessary, he said, to respect the principle of freedom of conscience — Christian as well as non-Christian — but it is no less so to protect the Republic. The two necessities being (as he considered) incompatible, he proposed to put the State first. Forcibly, but cynically, he likened the so-called "reform" of the religious Orders to a surgical operation performed without an anaesthetic. The operation might occasionally prove fatal — "for which of them I cannot say, but no doubt for some of them."

For one of them he proposed that it should prove fatal without delay. This "Order which has not been named," as he put it, and which he proposed to kill outright, takes a vow of obedience to an authority other than the State. Everybody knew what he meant, and the announcement "I mean the Jesuits" caused no sensation. Of the Society of Jesus he would make an example. The Jesuits must go.

As to the remainder of the proposals, Sr. Azaña admitted that they were illiberal and regretted that he was "going to shock Liberal opinion." But there must be no half-measures. Earlier in the debate Sr. de los Ríos had spoken with some sympathy of the numerous Orders that engage in works of mercy, as well he might, for they have deserved well of all Spaniards. But would Sr. Azaña allow any exception to be made in their favour? Not for a moment. They proselytize, he cried, as well as nurse and heal. And proselytizing we cannot for a moment tolerate.

So the Orders are not to be allowed to engage in "business," whether it be the sale of embroidery and sweetmeats by nuns who devote their lives to doing good or the publication of learned journals and works of erudition by monks who include some of Spain's leading scholars. And, most serious matter of all, "not for a moment, at no time and under no conditions whatever" must the Orders be allowed to teach.

I greatly regret it, but this is necessary for the genuine defence of the Republic. . . . The continual influence of the religious Orders on the consciences of the young is precisely the secret of the situation through which Spain is now passing and which as Republicans — and not only as Republicans but as Spaniards — we are in duty bound, at all costs, to prevent. Do not tell me that this is contrary to freedom: it is a question of public health. Would you, who oppose this measure in the name of Liberalism, permit a university professor to lecture on Aristotle's astronomy and to say that the stars are fastened to spheres which make up the heavens? Would you permit sixteenth-century medicine to be taught from a Chair in a Spanish university? You would not; in spite of the professor's right to teach and in spite of his freedom of conscience, such a thing would certainly never be permitted. And I tell you that, in the sphere of the political and moral sciences, the Catholic religious Orders are compelled, by virtue of their dogma, to teach everything that is contrary to the principles which are the foundation of the modern State.

So Sr. Azaña went on. It was an all-night sitting, and, when the division was taken, at seven o'clock on the morning of the fourteenth, the article was approved by 178 votes to 59. Perhaps the most significant and striking fact which emerged from the announcement of the result was that, despite the importance of the question, almost half the members were absent or did not vote. Strange as it may seem, three members of the Government, Sres. Domingo, Albornoz and Lerroux, were absent, and as Sr. Alcalá Zamora [Prime Minister] and Sr. Maura [Minister of the Interior] voted with the opposition it can hardly be said that the Government gave enthusiastic support to its own proposals. At six o'clock that evening, notwithstanding the absence, as a sign of protest, of the Basque Catholics, there was a far fuller House than eleven hours earlier. The Prime Minister and the Home Secretary had had the courage of their convictions and had resigned. The situation was not an easy one. With unrest abroad in the country, a false step might be fatal to the Republic, yet there was no head of the State to appoint a new Prime Minister and no legal machinery for selecting one. Don Alejandro Lerroux, the senior member of the Government, which as a matter of course had announced its collective resignation, interpreted the feeling of the House in addressing its President, Professor Julián Besteiro, and asking him to act as though he were President of the Republic. As he signified his acceptance, the whole assembly, glad of an opportunity to relieve its pent-up emotions, rose like one man and cheered him to the echo.

"I shall not leave this House," cried Sr. Besteiro, "until the crisis is over."

"Long live the Republic!" cried Don Alejandro. "Long live Spain!"

"Long live the Republic and the Spanish nation!" responded Sr. Besteiro.

Once more the House rose to its feet and shouted *Vivas*.

In less than three hours, the crisis was over. As the Ministers trooped in and took their seats on the *banco azul* [government bench] it was at once observed that Sr. Azaña was at their head. Without great reluctance, it may safely be presumed, he had taken over the responsibilities to which the leading part he had played in bringing about the crisis had entitled him. A slight shuffling of personnel sufficed for the formation of a fresh Government, and in a brief speech the new Prime Minister announced that all was ready for pushing on with the Constitution.

The Asturian Revolution of October 1934

A. RAMOS-OLIVEIRA

The following selection provides a fairly reliable, though by no means definitive, account of the October, 1934, revolution. Sr. Ramos-Oliveira was an experienced journalist of leftwing Socialist sympathies. He was personally acquainted with many of the individuals and places mentioned in the chapter. This is the work, then, of an "insider," and it assumes that the reader has a general knowledge both of Spanish politics and of Marxism. In order to understand the chapter the reader should note carefully the author's use of adjectives in characterizing the several political parties and leaders; likewise his emphasis on the role, theoretical or actual, of social classes; and his use of Marxist categories throughout the interpretation.

His comments raise fundamental questions. To what extent is it correct to characterize the insurrection as a "defensive gesture"? What is the relationship between a moderate program and the use of violent means to achieve that program? Do persons and parties react primarily in terms of their "class interests"? To what extent was the insurrection a "moral victory" despite the total defeat of both the Asturian miners and the Catalan liberals? Finally, to what extent are the issues and emotions of the Civil War prefigured in the October, 1934, revolt?

THE CRISIS was foreseen. The Samper Government would present itself in the Cortes on the 1st of October, as stipulated by the Constitution. But Spain had so many ravages to reproach it with, that no one expected its continuation. Either it would be overthrown by the parliamentary majority or the President of the Republic would withdraw his confidence. During all the summer, in the midst of strikes, political crimes and menacing concentrations of Fascist and anti-Fascist crowds, this had been the unanimous conclusion of the political cabal. A speech made by the head of the C.E.D.A., Gil Robles, in which, without irony, he called Samper a "man of little tranquillizing influence at the head of the blue bench," brought down the Government as soon as Parliament resumed its sittings.

In this same speech, Gil Robles announced that his party would not support any Cabinet in which it was not represented. The President's dilemma was crystal clear: either to authorize a Government based on the parliamentary majority, or to dissolve the Cortes. But Alcalá Zamora clung obstinately to the idea of broadening still more the basis of the régime; he had already closed the constituent Parliament, and with a new dissolution of the Cortes his constitutional faculty in this direction would be exhausted; he would not be able to rid himself of the third Chamber.

The Republicans who made a parade of calling themselves moderates were mysteriously convinced that the President of the Republic would not admit the oligarchy to the Government; the Socialists vacillated in their prognostication. The moderate Republicans supposed that the President would dissolve the Cortes and that it would be they, in a Government of national concentration, who would *make* the elections. Socialist reticence was founded on the state of progressive opinion

From A. Ramos-Oliveira, *Politics, Economics, and Men of Modern Spain* (London, 1946), pp. 502–516. Reprinted by permission of A. Ramos-Oliveira.

in the country; they doubted whether Don Niceto would dare to defy it, especially as the Socialists had threatened revolution.

The crisis adjusted itself by the traditional process of those palace consultations where the President listened, or pretended to listen, to both Greeks and Trojans, according to the practice of the Spanish pseudo-constitutional monarchy. With Alcalá Zamora, no Ministerial crisis ever solved itself in less than a week.

All the Republicans — if one rightly exempts the Radicals from this nomenclature — advised the President to form a Government concentrating all the Republican elements except the Socialists, and to dissolve the Cortes. The Socialist Party promised, if the Government were entrusted to them, to form a homogeneous Government, purely Socialist in character, "so as to satisfy the justifiable anxieties of the working class which today is made a mock of." This was a purely theoretical attitude, but one which corresponded to a situation in which the Republicans did not want to be suspected of "Marxism" and the Socialists deplored the timidity of the Republicans.

Naturally there was no party loyal to the essential nature of the Republican régime which did not impress on the President the disastrous consequences which would arise from the admission of the C.E.D.A. or Popular Action to the new Government. And there were many outstanding men who reminded Alcalá Zamora of the tense expectancy of the working classes.

In spite of all this, it was known already on October 3rd that the President of the Republic would hand over the power to a Government based on the parliamentary majority in that factious Cortes. On the night of that same day, the order for the quartering of the troops was issued. The streets of Madrid were silent and deserted, except for the tramp of the soldiers bringing their mobilization orders to their officers; over the city lay the brooding calm which, as in nature, presages public disasters. The Socialist Committees were keeping their vigil.

The President's decision was proclaimed after only a few more hours' delay. By the middle of the evening of the 4th, Lerroux was once more Prime Minister, this time with three Ministers from the C.E.D.A.

On the following day, a general strike was proclaimed throughout Spain and bloody conflicts broke out in the north. On the 6th, the Government of the *Generalidad* rose and severed relations with the Madrid Government. And every Spanish Republican who was conscious of the issues at stake, saluted with grief, but also with resolute hope, the beginning of a tragedy which dislocated the tortuous designs of Catholic Fascism.

All the reputable Republican Parties condemned the way in which the President had solved the crisis. So did, in substance, the Basque Nationalist Party. These middle-class organizations were not revolutionary, nor did they take up arms like the proletariat, but they divorced themselves on the 5th of October from the corrupt institutions of the régime and, on moral grounds, they represented a cardinal factor in the insurrection.

The passive adhesion of the Republicans to the revolutionary movement took the form of several leaflets which reached the streets at the same time as the first exchange of shots between strikers and troops. The Republican Left (Azaña) declared that "the monstrous deed of handing over the Government of the Republic to its enemies is treason" and stated that they "broke off all relations with the present institutions of the régime and affirmed their decision to adopt all means to defend the Republic," *Unión Republicana* (Martínez Barrio) argued that the entry of the C.E.D.A. into the Government obliged it to "sever all collaboration and withdraw all support from the organs of the régime." The *Partido Republicano Conservador* (Miguel Maura, ex-colleague in the Republic of Alcalá Zamora) proclaimed that "hastily and forgetful of all, we are being expelled from our legal position in the Republic" and affirmed "from now on, our essential incompatibility with this sullied Republic, ante-room of a brutal and anti-democratic reaction."

Other small parties of the Left issued similar protests. And the Valencian public must have displayed a certain bewilderment before a paragraph in *El Pueblo,* organ of the Samper Party, which stated that "faced with a period of oppression and shame, no other way remains than the revolutionary volley." Samper himself was Minister of Foreign Affairs in the new Government!

What should perhaps most urgently claim our attention now is the grouping of the social classes in the October conflict. Whenever a decisive political crisis arises in Spain, two national nuclei form themselves spontaneously — the agrarian oligarchy on the one hand and the historic middle class and the proletariat on the other; incontrovertible proof, let us repeat, of the existence of powerful common interests between the Spanish *bourgeoisie* and proletariat, as opposed to the upper classes; and proof also that, if afterwards the progressive nucleus disintegrates, it is due to a lack of clear vision of the national problem among the democratic classes and the want of a man, or men, capable of gathering together and transmuting into action the common sentiment. At bottom, the October revolution is only a reproduction, attuned to other circumstances, of the revolutionary movements of 1917 and 1930. And the survival of the agrarian-aristocratic oligarchy, which neither of those movements succeeded in destroying, however much they weakened or undermined the monarchy, is the *ultima ratio* [final, underlying reason] of the bloody events of 1934.

The rise to power of the agrarian oligarchy provoked anew the *rapprochement* of industrialists, merchants and proletariat in the political arena. Although they were both ardently Catholic, the Castilian-Andalusian agrarian oligarchy and the Basque agrarian and industrial middle class were bound to clash, and, in spite of the fact that the Basque Nationalist Party took care not to appear revolutionary, the aggression against the Economic Agreement, prelude to other aggressions, urged it forward towards the lines of the anti-oligarchic opposition. The same thing happened with the Catalan *Lliga.* The *Lliga* had taken up its stand with the Samper Government long before the heralded revolution was taken seriously. And it was inevitable that this should happen, though the Catalan capitalists accepted the situation with a wry face; for when the *Lliga* was defeated in the elections for the Catalan Parliament and its interests attacked by the *Esquerra,* only from the Samper Government could it hope for a salve to assuage, even slightly, the onslaught of the *Generalidad.* Fleeing from the enemy at his heels, Cambó sought refuge in Samper (that is to say, in Gil Robles) and supported him in Parliament in exchange for concessions like the appeal against the *Ley de Contratos de cultivo.*[1] If the *Lliga* had been in power in Catalonia, it would certainly have been in conflict with the Samper Government, like the Basque nationalists; but as the Samper Government was its only stay and prop, it supported it, though grudgingly, in the Cortes. And when Cambó realized that the October crisis would be solved by the entry into the Government of three Ministers from the *C.E.D.A.,* he declared, alluding to his party's attitude, that as the new Government did, so would they do. That is, the *Lliga* accepted the majority Cabinet of October 4th with the mistrust with which the great industrialists had always viewed the great landowners in power.

When the workers' rebellion had been quelled and the Cortes resumed its tasks

---

[1] A law intended to give the tenant farmers of Catalonia an opportunity to buy land which they had worked as tenants for a number of years. Catalan conservatives got the Tribunal of Constitutional Guarantees to declare this land reform law unconstitutional. It was public knowledge that the issue was more political and social than legal. [Editor's note.]

on November 5th, the *Lliga* voted its confidence in the Government with obvious displeasure and then only after Lerroux had announced that he would not be surprised if the proletarian rising repeated itself — an absurd suspicion.

Two important lessons can be learnt from the period of history after 1917. The first is that the class struggle in the regions of the industrial *bourgeoisie,* that is, in the Basque Provinces and Catalonia, renders the prosperity of regional autonomies impossible from every point of view and makes of separatism a utopian creed. Because whoever governs in Madrid, the class which has been displaced by the autonomous Government will lean, at the expense of the class which has been brought to the top, upon the centralizing forces of the rest of Spain. And the second lesson is that, in a régime of constitutional liberty, the class struggle between proletariat and *bourgeoisie* frustrates the possibility of establishing a front capable of changing the basic form of oligarchic government in favour of a national democracy, whether agrarian or *bourgeois,* or even a working-class democracy. Hence, it is in the interests of all the progressive classes in Spain to suppress or to mitigate the political differences which divide them, in order to emphasize what distinguishes them in common from the aristocratic-agrarian-financial oligarchy. Naturally, it is absurd to suppose this could be realized at one blow in a system of civil liberty and universal suffrage. But it is not less certain that, if Spaniards could be convinced that the parliamentary path will always lead to civil war in Spain in the present relationship of the classes, the work of the statesman would be greatly lightened.

In 1934 the Liberal Republic had failed in Spain, as it failed in Russia in October 1917. But Spain's political frontiers are very different from the political frontiers of Russia; and as the international situation in 1917 helped Lenin, so the international situation in 1934 helped the Spanish Fascist parties. But the Spanish revolution

of October was, before all, a defensive gesture. However radical the revolutionary propaganda of the working-class parties appeared — a radicalism imposed by the oligarchy which, in resisting every reform, impelled the masses to a desperate extremism — however radical this propaganda may have appeared, none of the proletarian parties had any other thought than to re-establish the popular Republic as it had been conceived, in its social aspect, before the 14th of April, 1931. . . .

The political-social programme of the insurgents, which was not made public until fifteen months after the events of October, gives the measure of the policy the Socialist Party and its associates were pursuing. It consists of ten points, which can be summarized as follows: (1) Nationalization of the land, which was to become State property, except in the regions of the small-holdings where it was to remain in the possession of the actual cultivators; all land rents to be collected by the State, the municipalities or other public communities or corporations authorized by the State; in the regions of the latifundia, collective cultivation to be established; (2) progressive acceleration of hydraulic works and, in consideration of the fact that the supplies voted in the Budget were inadequate, use to be made of the national savings at a moderate rate of interest. "This operation could be carried out through a partnership between the State, the federative entity of the *Cajas de Ahorro* [savings banks] and official banking, mortgaging the lands which were capable of irrigation": (3) higher education to be reserved exclusively for pupils who had reached a satisfactory standard in the elementary and secondary schools; special schools to be created to complete the technical knowledge of the workers and raise their general cultural level: (4) dissolution of all the religious orders and confiscation of their property, plus the expulsion of the Jesuits from the national territory: (5) disbandment of the Army, reduction of its contingents and recruitment of men and officers from among the parties loyal to the Republic; those who had shown whole-hearted adhesion to the régime to be allowed to remain in the Army: (6) dissolution of the Civil Guard and reorganization of the police forces on the same democratic bases as the Army: (7) modification of all the organs of the Public Administration and weeding out of officials hostile to the Republic: (8) the moment not being propitious for carrying out the socialization of the major part of Spanish industry, the programme to be confined to measures for the moral and material betterment of the workers, allowing them to share in the control of those industrial organizations in which they were employed: (9) reform of the taxation system, special emphasis being laid on taxes on unearned income and inheritance: (10) the foregoing programme to be carried out rapidly by decree and endorsed later by legislative organs freely ordained by the people; "and in the belief that this programme would not obtain the assent of the present occupant of the Presidential chair, steps would be taken to relieve him of his office."

As can be seen, if the October revolution had achieved its final objective, the Republic would not have gone much farther than it was intended to go at birth. In fact, only the agrarian oligarchy would have suffered gravely in its interests. And it seems beyond doubt that, on the basis of such a programme, a national movement of democracy versus oligarchy could have been formed, if there had been anyone to initiate it or any understanding of realities among the Republican and working-class parties. The Spanish bourgeoisie, including the great industrial capitalists, would have gained rather than lost by the nationalization of the great agrarian properties, the hydraulic works and other economic reforms.

These, then, were the political and social aspirations of the October combatants, or the Workers' Alliance.

In almost the whole of Spain, the distinctive tendencies of the proletarian movement had been united in a revolutionary coalition to resist Fascism. In Asturias, the interpenetration of Socialists, Communists and Anarchist-Trade Unionists was complete. Not so in Catalonia, where, because the C.N.T. was more closely controlled by the F.A.I., this popular sector remained on the fringe of the Workers' Alliance.

The revolution spread over the whole of Spain, but with significant lack of uniformity. Except in Barcelona, the Republicans registered a platonic protest in the rest of the country. The peasants did not fight, except in isolated villages of Andalusia, Castile, Navarre and Aragon. The June strike had prostrated the agrarian movement and its effects were felt in October. But the miners of the north — Asturias, Viscaya, León, Santander, Palencia — fought heroically. With few exceptions, military discipline did not crack for a single moment. The proletariat of the great cities did not raise their rebellion much above the level of a general strike. In some towns they did not even stop work; in others, the general strike lasted twenty-four, forty-eight hours. In Madrid the strike lasted nine days and the revolution was not a rising of the masses which imperils the State, but a spasmodic disturbance which harasses the police.

From the 5th to the 13th October inclusive there was a unanimous strike in Madrid. The proletariat gave a marked impression of discipline and resistance. The strike began in the early hours of Friday the 5th. The Government thought that on Saturday the workers would go back to work, driven by the necessity of drawing their week's wages. This did not happen; and then the authorities conceived the hope that the workers would go back to work on Monday. They were soon disabused. On Monday, it was clear from the spirit of the workers that the strike would go on for at least a week. Most of the railwaymen had stopped work, although they were as a rule difficult to draw into a revolutionary strike. On the West and M.Z.A. lines, the workers left their posts in a body and the Government was obliged to mobilize the first and second Railway Reserves. Moreover there occurred in Madrid frequent clashes between strikers and police, bomb explosions, petards, etc.

In the great capitals the people were psychologically prepared for a political, anti-Fascist strike, but not for a fight to overcome the Government. The necessary conditions for social revolution were wanting; and the proletariat lacked arms. But as a political strike, that in Madrid was a splendid sample of civic maturity.

The insurrection in Asturias — comparable with the Paris Commune — can be explained by the revolutionary temper of the miners, who possess one of the oldest and most seasoned Socialist organizations; by the material and strategic possibilities; by the relative weakness of the Government forces, and by the unanimity with which all the workers plunged into the revolution. The Asturian miners have always responded to all insurrections with terrific impetus. In 1917 it was these same Asturian miners who gave the most trouble to the Government troops. In 1934 the revolution in Asturias was a rising of the masses, a social revolution. The miners were joined by the industrial proletariat and by a motley crowd of peasants, whose presence was explained by the fact that the miners raised levies in all the villages of the mining valley where they passed, snatching away useful men. *"Hala! camaradas!"* was their rallying cry. Thus was formed a torrential flood, which swept away the posts of the Civil Guard, set up a new social order, born of the moment and embodying the social ideas predominating in each zone, and passed on to spread towards Oviedo or distribute itself over the mountains. Having overcome the resistance of the Civil Guard and taken their arms, the miners marched in a column on the Asturian capital, into which they penetrated, without military advice worthy of the name, firing off sticks of dynamite which they lighted with their cigars. Five, six or seven thousand warlike men, accustomed to the most arduous labour and the cruellest dangers, fought valiantly in the streets of the city, most of which they occupied during nine terrible days.

To suppress the Asturian insurrection, the Lerroux-Gil Robles Government sent by sea from Spanish Morocco the *Tercio Extranjero* [Foreign Legion], a shock force which the monarchy had wanted to use in 1930 to quell the Republican movement. The proposal to move these troops, who had been formed to fight the Moors, to the Peninsula, was sharply censured at the time by Alcalá Zamora himself. But where the monarchy did not succeed, the Republic did. And in 1934 the Government did not stop at bringing up a few *banderas* [c.600 men per *bandera*] of the *Tercio*; they also sent to Asturias two *tabores* [c.225 men per *tabor*] of regulars or Moorish troops. In this way, the Berbers made their appearance in lands that they had never been able to trample underfoot. Mahometans now made war on Spaniards at the command of a Government which was half Catholic, half masonic. But the oligarchy had already given clear proofs that it would stick at nothing if it saw its property menaced; it felt itself so weak, so devoid of moral and material authority to sustain an unjust Government, that already in 1934 it began to have recourse to outside help, to the use of foreign forces — a policy which was to culminate in the civil war, when besides relying on the *Tercio* and the Moors, who were quickly defeated by the Republican militias, it was to open the frontiers of Spain to the regular troops of other nations.

For the Republicans, Catalonia was the last bastion of the Republic. Ruled by a middle-class Government which would not compound with the entry of the *C.E.D.A.* into the Government, Catalonia promised to be, in October 1934, the invincible redoubt of democracy. Like the Basque nationalists, the *Esquerra* had withdrawn from the Cortes and the *Generalidad* had been in a state of rebellion since the verdict on the *Ley de Contratos de cultivo*.

The directors of Catalan Left policy found themselves, on the eve of the event, in the same state of mind as the Socialist and Republican leaders. They prepared to face the delicate circumstances which would be created by the formation of a Ministry with politicians who were not acceptable to the popular Republic. But they could not imagine the thing would really happen. The President of the *Generalidad,* like Azaña, like the moderate Republicans, envisaged the possibility of a Government based on the parliamentary majority with the anxiety caused by things which *may* happen, which may easily happen, but which, owing to the consequences they are bound to entail, usually remain stillborn.

At midday on the 4th, that is, hours before the Ministerial crisis had been solved, the President of the Catalan Government tried to establish communication with the President of the Republic. He did not succeed, but he spoke over the telephone to Sánchez Guerra, Secretary-General of the Presidency of the Republic. Companys asked him to inform His Excellency that the Government of the *Generalidad* would send him a telegram announcing that the admission of the *C.E.D.A.* to the Government would precipitate a catastrophe in Catalonia. At three o'clock in the afternoon, Sánchez Guerra rang up President Companys and told him: "His Excellency begs you not to worry and reiterates his affection towards yourself and his respect for your Government." The fact is that, up to the last moment, Alcalá Zamora was giving the Republicans the impression that no one would be made a Minister unless he had expressly declared himself in favour of Republicanism.

By mid-afternoon of the 4th, the list of the new Cabinet was known in Barcelona. In the Palace of the *Generalidad,* the news came like a thunderbolt. The hour of great decisions had struck; but the men

of the *Esquerra* wavered. They feared that the proletariat, the Workers' Alliance and the *F.A.I.* would control the revolution. And while Companys, before rising in rebellion, assured the Catalan people that there, in the Government, stood the defenders of their liberties, Dencás, the Minister of the Interior, summoned the political chiefs and warned them: "Watch the *F.A.I.*" The Catalan middle class was now going through the phase which the Madrid middle class, the Mauras and the Martínez Barrios, had already gone through; fearful that the Republic would escape them through the Left, they did everything in their power to destroy it through the Right.

The night of the 4th passed and the whole of the 5th, without Catalonia coming to a decision. In the rest of Spain, the working classes were carrying on the fight in one way or another. The Republicans had issued their statements of policy. And public opinion was asking: What is the *Generalidad* waiting for? At last, on the 6th, the leaders of the *Esquerra* agreed to rise against the Madrid Government.

The revolutionary movement decreed from Madrid by the workers' centres, except the Anarchists', was, until the night of the 6th, in Barcelona, a general peaceful strike. There it was the Government which had promised to open fire. Consequently, though perhaps with hesitation, President Companys appeared on the balcony of the *Generalidad* in the early hours of the night of the 6th and proclaimed the Catalan State of the Federal Spanish Republic — an absurd, but typical, proceeding.

The phases of the revolution in Catalonia can be summarized as follows: A night of shelling of the buildings of the *Generalidad.* Barricades. Heavy shooting in the streets. The Catalan Councillors resisted the fire of the troops, waiting for the *rabassaires,*[2] the "brothers of the Maresma, of Tarrasa, Hospitalet, Sans," who did not

[2] Strongly unionized tenant farmers in the Catalan vineyards. [Editor's note.]

come. At dawn, Companys and his colleagues in the Ministry surrendered to General Batet. Dencás fled.

As in the rest of Spain, except the mining valleys of the north, the masses in Catalonia seemed to be inhibited. Not only did the Anarchists not fight, but on the 8th of October, they asked the military authorities for permission to broadcast an order terminating the general strike. They did much the same thing in other capitals, where they hastened to assure the Governor that they had nothing to do with the revolution. Now, as during Azaña's Government and in December 1933, during the Lerroux Government, the conduct of the Anarchists — except in Asturias — coincided, no doubt fortuitously, with the interests of the aristocracy.

The losses occasioned by the entry of the C.E.D.A. into the Government — the cause of the rebellion — were considerable, both in lives and property. The central districts of Oviedo were devastated, the University building with its magnificent library was burnt down, and the cathedral, where the Government troops were posted, suffered some damage.

The number of dead throughout Spain was 1,335 and the wounded 2,951, most of them peasants, that is, insurgents. After October, about 40,000 persons were thrown into prisons and penitentiaries.

But not all the revolutionaries fell fighting; many were murdered by the forces charged with suppressing the conflict, after it had already ceased. For once the rebellion was extinguished, although some combatants still remained dispersed in the Asturian mountains, the repressive measures were ruthless and the arbitrary punishment of Asturias by the African troops was carried out with a total disregard for the letter and spirit of the law. And these new horrors, coming on top of the disasters of the struggle, dealt a deathblow to Spanish Fascism in its cradle.

Police repression was characterized by unbounded severity — but it was symptomatic that *political* repression failed. Even

though defeated, the people had succeeded in their primary objective. The revolutionary movement of October altered the whole political calendar of the C.E.D.A., dislocating its plans for the pacific conquest of the Government. The repressive measures which the oligarchy was preparing against the time when, advancing from post to post, it would deprive the Socialists of honour, prestige and mass support, were still premature.

For its part, the aristocratic party demanded draconian measures. How this party wished, like Caligula, that the people had only one head! They would have liked the heads of the Socialist leaders, the dissolution of all the non-Fascist parties, the confiscation of the funds of the trade unions, the closing of the Cortes — in short, an implacable dictatorship. Political repression was confined to the suspension of the Socialist Press, a declaration that the Asturian Miners' Trade Union was illegal and the taking over of certain *Casas del Pueblo*[3] to house the Government forces. The workers' organizations, both political and trade-unionist, continued firmly in existence, more firmly than they would have been had the workers accepted without a protest and without sacrifice a Government which was but a prelude to Fascism. From the attack, the Government passed over to the defence, in the face of the universal execration it had aroused for having brought the Moors to Spain and for the excesses committed by the expeditionary forces which invaded Asturias. The oligarchy was not able to instal an even more abominable dictatorship than the one Spanish democracy had endured under the Samper Government.

The C.E.D.A. and its offshoots did not expect that the revolution would assume the dimensions it did. They thought that it would not pass beyond the stage of a twenty-four-hour general strike — this was the thesis put forward by *El Debate* —

[3] Trade union headquarters, often including modest library and recreational facilities. [Editor's note.]

and that once the Socialists had heard the crack of the whip, they could deal with them later with a heavy hand à la Dollfuss. This had happened in Vienna, because Social-Democratic Austria had lost a critical year, and when afterwards it plucked up courage to resist, the Catholic party completely controlled the State and had already made its decisive stroke; and while in February 1934 the Socialist militias of the *Schutzbund* were fighting, in Vienna everyone was working — an extraordinary spectacle; not even the working classes were on strike. The danger in Spain was the same — that the proletariat would become demoralized for lack of wise and dynamic leadership, and would become Fascist, or, at least, cease to be Socialist. But October prevented this. The ones who were demoralized were the Fascist parties.

On the other hand, there can be no doubt that, before the October explosion, the Vatican, becoming terrified by the turn of political events, had finally convinced itself of the perils which a totalitarian dictatorship in Spain would bring on the Church, with the various factions fighting each other tooth and nail. Paradoxically enough, the Holy See insisted upon the *C.E.D.A.* acting with greater tact and prudence. Austrian Catholic Fascism had fallen into the crass error of destroying Social-Democracy, the only popular force really opposed to the native Nazis, who, thinking they had as much right as Dollfuss to seize the Government with violence, had tried to do so in July by assassinating the "pocket Chancellor." Rome had reached the point of being persuaded — and the sight of the Spanish cataclysm finally convinced her — that by relying on brute force, the Spanish Catholics were setting a pernicious example which might be imitated by Conservative parties which were not the party of the Church.

After the October insurrection, Gil Robles learnt to moderate his political language. The perplexity and moderation which may be observed now in the speeches of the head of the *C.E.D.A.* are at odds with the arrogance and aggressiveness of his former political declarations. For example, Gil Robles had said in Madrid on October 15th, 1933, a year before the revolution: "We want the whole Government and that is what we are asking for. To realize this ideal, we are not going to be restrained by archaic forms. Democracy is for us not an end in itself, but a means whereby we go forward to conquer the new State. When this moment arrives, Parliament will either submit or we shall sweep it away." Compare this paragraph with the following, of November 20th, 1934: "Confronted with the excesses of political Liberalism, there has little by little arisen in the world . . . a doctrinal current, subsequently embodied in political systems, which leads directly to the absorption by the State of all individual activities. The sum and compendium of such a totalitarian doctrine is the celebrated phrase of Mussolini: 'Everything in the State, nothing against the State, nothing outside the State.' Against this political current" — adds Gil Robles — "which is gaining a hold in youth circles, it seems to me necessary to react."

The bloodshed of October which cemented the union of the Spanish working classes, sowed disunity, on the other hand, among the ranks of the conquerors. The Monarchists, in particular, thought there would never again be such a favourable moment for a *coup d'état.* But for the agrarian-Catholics, such aristocratic impatience was the alpha and omega of irresponsibility and demagogy.

With the Republicans out of the fight, national policy was divided, in dramatic monopoly, between three forces in collision — the President of the Republic, the *C.E.D.A.* and *Renovación Española* [Monarchist party]. The President, seriously perturbed by the catastrophe he had so frivolously precipitated, and morally prostrated, showed nevertheless rare integrity in the face of possible new dangers. The shock of October had forced Don Niceto to awake to realities. A *coup d'état* was to be feared, although the skirmishing in the oligarchic camp diminished, if it did not destroy, the menace. The President of the Republic, in any case, prepared to save what remained of the régime. He placed generals who were in his confidence where they could be useful and personally supervised from his high position the movements of troops. The officers who were hostile to the Republic had not risen this time, and, if they had intended to, their intention was largely frustrated by the resolute action of Álcala Zamora, who might well have been surprised later by a military *coup* if the popular rising had not occurred in October.

The subsequent political events can be summarized as follows. The President of the Republic refused to sanction or to sign any death warrants, particularly the death sentence passed on the leader of the Asturian miners, Ramón González Peña; and with the struggle which arose on this count between the Right *bloc* and Alcalá Zamora, the discord in the oligarchic camp grew. The Monarchists reproached the *Cedists* for staying in a "soft" Government which did not proceed against the revolutionary chiefs with the inexorability they thought the occasion merited. And Gil Robles, between the plutocratic Charybdis and the Presidential Scylla, lost for some time his authority over those social classes which saw with malevolent disgust how the opportunity for striking off the most prominent Socialist heads was being lost. The *C.E.D.A.* chief found himself in an impossible situation. Aristocratic extremism threatened to leave him without a party if he temporized with the President of the Republic, but the President of the Republic was holding the sword of Damocles over the head of the Cortes.

Gil Robles understood, nevertheless, that he had without delay, to offer his defrauded followers authentic proof of his Ministerial power and he made it a point of honour to see that the sentences passed by the military tribunals were carried out. Firmness in this dispute, however, did but show up the impotence of the *C.E.D.A.*, although it enabled it, at least, to save its face before that part of the public which was opposed to clemency. The Government which had provoked the revolution fell, then, on March 29th, 1935. On April 3rd, Lerroux formed a homogeneous Cabinet of Radicals, which did not even get as far as appearing before the Cortes, and at the beginning of May, after a month of arduous negotiation, the *C.E.D.A.* declared itself resolved to re-enter the Government. Gil Robles announced his claim to lead the new Ministry, but the President did not view the project with sympathy. In the end the Catholics agreed to accept five portfolios, two more than in the first majority Cabinet, and Alcalá Zamora had no scruples in augmenting the *C.E.D.A.* contingent since he brought into the Government as Minister of the Interior Portela Valladares, an old and astute politician, very much to the President's taste. Gil Robles took over the War Office himself, appointed General Franco Under-Secretary, and raised the hopes of the enemies of the Republic out of all proportion to the situation. The Catholics did not achieve any more in the War Office than a Señor Hidalgo would have done, if he had been pressed. And the understandable irresolution of Gil Robles or the intemperate haste of his competitors in the oligarchic camp could not but inflame still more every day the intestine strife of the plutocratic parties.

. . . It is fitting that this chapter should end on this note — sixteen months later, the popular Republic was to arise, like another phoenix, from the ashes of October.

Political Cleavages in a Castilian Village, Summer 1935

ARTURO BAREA

Arturo Barea was one of many Spanish intellectuals and professional men who joined the Socialist Party in the early days of the Republic. He had a small summer home near Madrid, and in the village of Novés his economic and professional standing placed him with the rich men, whereas his Socialist affiliations placed him with the poor. The following selection from Barea's autobiography deals with village politics in the summer of 1935, after the Asturian revolt and repression, and before the election which brought the Popular Front to power. The reader will want to consider to what extent the attitudes reflected in Barea's report confirm or refute the concept of "class interest." He will also wish to compare Barea's description of Novés with Brenan's description of an Andalusian village. Finally, may the hints of black-mail and threatened violence have helped to prepare the people of Spain to accept the coming of civil war as inevitable?

N OVÉS LIES at the bottom of a ravine scooped out of the plain, and is built on the pattern of a fish's spine. There is a very wide main street, through the middle of which flows a stream blackened by the refuse of the whole village. On both sides, short alleys like ribs lead up the steep, rough slopes. When it rains, the bottom of the ravine becomes the bed of a torrent which sluices away the heaped-up muck. Then people are forced to use the bridges which span the whole width of the street at intervals. One of them is high, humpbacked, made of fitted stones; it is Roman. Another is of concrete and the road passes over it. Most of the houses are built of sun-baked clay with a thick coat of whitewash. They all look alike and they all implacably reflect the glare of the sun. There is a square with a few small trees, the church, the apothecary, the Casino, and the Town Hall. And that is all there is of Novés: some two hundred houses.

I followed the dirty brook downstream, because I had nothing else to do. After the last small houses, the ravine opened into a valley sheltered from the winds of the plain and gently green even in August. On both sides of the stream were market gardens with fruit trees, flowers, and vegetable plots. Each garden had its own well and chain pump. A slight murmur of water and clanking of iron was in the air all the time. A mile further on the valley folded up and the little river ran again through a barren ravine sunk into the arid, dusty plain. This was the whole wealth of Novés. Walking back, I noted that most of the chain pumps were silent, and remembered that it was Sunday. But then I began to see more. Many of the garden plots lay abandoned or badly neglected. There were a few small beds of melons which had been cared for, but the big market-gardens looked as though nobody had worked there for months. The earth was baked in hard lumps. I looked down a well-shaft by the wayside. The chain with the buckets was rusty, green weeds floated on the water. Nobody had used the pump for a very

From Arturo Barea, *The Forging of a Rebel* (New York, 1946), pp. 427–436. Reprinted by permission of the Barea estate.

long time. Back at my house, I talked to Mariano about it. His answer was to the point.

"It's a sin against God, that's what it is. The men without work, and the land abandoned. You won't believe it, but something's going to happen here, something nasty. It's been like this for the last three years, almost as long as we've had the Republic."

"But how's that? I know the big landowners are refusing to employ labor nowadays, but here in the village, I didn't think there were any big landowners."

"We've only got four rich men in the village. Things wouldn't go so badly if it weren't for Heliodoro. The others aren't really bad. But Heliodoro has got them all where he wants them, and there's a war on all the time."

He was no longer taciturn, and his gray eyes came alive in his heavy face.

"I'll tell you something of what's going on here. Before the Republic came, some of our young people joined the Socialists and some joined the Anarchists, well, less than a dozen in all. I don't know how they had the guts to do it, because the Civil Guards were after them all the time and beat them up often enough. But of course, when the Republic came, the Corporal of the Civil Guard had to lie low at first, and a lot of us joined. Nearly the whole village is with the Socialists or Anarchists now. But Heliodoro has always been the boss here and managed the elections for the deputy of Torrijos. And so now he's doing what he's always done, because before the Republic he was sometimes a Liberal and sometimes a Conservative, but never on the wrong side. And when the Republic came, well, then he joined Lerroux's crowd and now, because the Right's been getting strong after what happened in Asturias, he's become one of Gil Robles' crowd. And when our lads asked for decent wages Heliodoro got the four rich men of the village together and said to them: 'Those rascals must be taught a lesson.' So then they started chucking people out

and only giving work to the ones who swallowed the old conditions. Because there are some like that, too. And then, you know how things happen in a village, most of us have a bit of land and there's always something the matter with the wife, or the garden gets flooded by the rains, and so lots of people owe Heliodoro money. And because he's the man whose word goes in the village, he got hold of the Municipal Secretary and the Mayor and took out papers against everyone so that he could keep their land. And so things are getting ugly. They were ugly two years ago. People went and messed up the gardens. But now it's worse, because now it's the other side that has the power."

"And the young people, what about them?"

"What d'you suppose they could do? Keep their mouths shut and tighten their belts. When things happened in Asturias[1] two or three of them were taken away, and now nobody dares to say a word. But something will happen some fine day. Heliodoro won't die in his bed."

"Have you got Trade Unions here, then?"

"We've got nothing. The men meet at Eliseo's. He's got a tavern and he's turned it into a Workers' Casino, and there they talk. Eliseo went and joined the Anarchists out there in the Argentine."

"I suppose you've got a club secretary, or something of the kind?"

[1] The various references to events in Asturias in this and the following chapters allude to the events of October 1934, when the workers' associations called a general strike, which was followed by revolutionary risings in Asturias, Barcelona, and Madrid, so as to prevent the coming to power of the right-wing leader Gil Robles and his party, the C.E.D.A. (Confederación Española de Derechas Autónomas), with a clearly Fascist program. The armed rising of the Asturian miners, stronger than the other abortive movements, was suppressed by General Ochoa's Legionaries and Moors, then for the first time used on the soil of the Peninsula and against Spaniards. The ensuing violent measures of oppression during the "Two Black Years" (Bienio Negro) roused public indignation to such a degree that Gil Robles was never called upon to form a Government. [Author's note.]

"We haven't got a thing. What the men do is to meet and talk. Because nobody wants trouble with the Corporal."

"I must go and have a look at your Casino."

"You can't go there, sir. It's only for the poor. You've got a Casino in the market square, that's for the gentry."

"I'll go there, too."

"Well, then, they'll chuck you out of one or the other, sir, to be sure."

"And what are you a member of, Mariano?"

"I hope you won't get annoyed, but it's like this: When the Republic came, the same thing happened to me as to the others, we were all for it, and I joined the Trade Union — the U.G.T. But there, you see, it hasn't helped us much, to tell you the truth."

"I'm a member of the U.G.T., too."

"The devil you are." Mariano stared at me with great seriousness, "What a mess! Well, you've got yourself into a tight spot here!"

"We shall see. I don't expect the Corporal will beat me up."

"You never know."

In the afternoon, Mariano and I went to the "Poor Men's Casino," as he called it. The place was a former stable, a huge room with crossbeams, a billiard table in the middle, a small bar at the back, and a score of scratched tables along the bare walls. An ancient radio set built on sham Gothic lines stood in a corner. The billiard table fascinated me; I could not imagine how it ever landed in Novés. It had eight elephantine legs, and eight men could have slept comfortably on its top. The cloth was riddled with tears drawn together with twine. Apparently the table was used for everything, even for an occasional game of billiards; a match was just going on, in which the twine and chance directed the balls. Mariano led me to the bar.

"Give us something to drink, Eliseo."

The man behind the bar filled two glasses with wine without saying a word. There were about forty people in the room. Suddenly I tumbled to the fact that they had all fallen silent and were watching us. Eliseo stared straight into my eyes. At the first glance, his face gave you a shock. An ulcer had gnawed away one of his nostrils, and a few hairs were sticking out between the livid, greenish seams of the wound. It looked like a biblical, a medieval sore. But the curious thing was that the man was so detached from his blemish that he provoked neither pity nor physical revulsion. Eliseo was in the middle forties, short and squat, dark, sun-tanned, with quick, shrewd eyes and a sensual mouth. The way in which he looked me up and down while he drank a sip of wine was a provocation. When I set down my empty glass, he said:

"And you, why have you come here? This is the Workers' Casino, and if you hadn't been with Mariano, I wouldn't have served you."

Mariano intervened:

"Don Arturo is one of us, he belongs to the U.G.T."

"Is that true?"

I handed Eliseo the membership card of my Trade Union. He scanned every page and then called out:

"Boys, Don Arturo is a comrade!" He turned to me: "When we heard you were coming here we all said: 'Another son of a bitch, as if we hadn't enough of them anyhow!'"

He left his corner behind the bar to join me, and in the center of the clustering men I had to report on events in Madrid: how the Right was organizing and how the Left was coming to life again after the "Black Year" of repression. The wine was cheap, the drinks were on me and they began to talk. There were great hopes and great plans. The Left would come back into the Government and things would be different this time. The rich would have to choose between paying decent wages and giving up their land so that the others could work it. Novés would have a big communal market garden with a lorry of its own, which would carry greens and fruit to Madrid every morning. And they would finish the school building.

"The scoundrels!" said Eliseo. "Have you seen our school? The Republic put up the money for it and they sent us a beautiful drawing from Madrid of a house with big windows and a garden. But Heliodoro and his gang convinced the Madrid gentlemen that the school should be built out in the plain, above the valley. And there they started building. Heliodoro got a lot of money for the site, which was his, of course, and up there in the dust you can see the four unfinished walls."

"Next time we'll build it ourselves, down in the orchards. They're so beautiful, it's a real blessing from God," said another.

"You can't imagine, Don Arturo," said Eliseo, "how glad I am that you're one of us. Now we'll show them that we aren't just a few poor yokels. But you'll have to look out. They'll try to get you."

That evening I went to the "Rich Men's Casino."

There was the obligatory big saloon with marble-topped tables and men drinking coffee or coffee-and-brandy, a billiard table, and a tobacco-laden atmosphere, and behind it a smaller room crowded with card players. A plump little man, womanish in voice, skin, and gestures, made a beeline for me:

"Good evening, Don Arturo, that's right, you've come to join us, haven't you? You already know our Heliodoro, don't you?" I knew the tight-lipped man to whose table I was gently propelled. He was my landlord. The plump little man babbled on: "Excuse me for a tiny little moment, I've got to get the coffee ready, you know, but I won't be long." Everything was arranged for me. Heliodoro introduced me to the two black-coated men at his table —

"Our two doctors, Don Julián and Don Anselmo" — and asked me the obvious questions: had I settled down, had the move been difficult, and so forth. I have never been good at small talk, and this was as boring as any. The effeminate little man brought coffee and asked me the same questions all over again, until one of the doctors cut him short:

"José, enter Don Arturo in the list."

José produced a fat leather-bound notebook and thumbed it, giving me a glimpse of pages filled with columns of figures and headed by names.

"Now, let's see. How many are there in your family?"

"But surely I won't have to enter all my children as members of the Casino!"

"Oh, this hasn't anything to do with the Casino. This is our local Medical Aid Association. I put you on the list and it gives you a right to medical assistance whenever you need it."

"But I've got a doctor in Madrid."

Don Julián grunted:

"All right, if you don't want it, we won't put you down. But I warn you, if you've an urgent case in your family and you aren't a subscriber, my colleague here will send you a nice little bill. If you've a splinter in your thumb and he lances it, he'll put it down as 'for a surgical operation, two hundred pesetas.'"

"And if I call you in?"

"It's he who makes out the bills in any case. It would come to the same thing."

"All right, then, put me down. My wife, four children, and myself. Six in all."

"In what category, please, Don Julián?"

"Don't ask obvious questions, José. In our category, of course."

"Five pesetas per month, Don Arturo. And what about your servant?"

"Isn't she a member of your Association already?"

"Well, yes, she's on our list, but she doesn't pay. So she's been struck off. And if she has an accident at work, you'll have to pay."

Don Julián sniggered:

"Say she burns her hand on the frying-pan. For a surgical operation and treatment, two hundred pesetas."

"Put the servant down, then."

"Two pesetas. D'you want to pay now? I'm the cashier. It won't take me a second to make out the receipts."

José pocketed the seven pesetas and tripped away, to reappear with a pack of cards.

"One hundred pesetas in the bank, this deal."

He went straight into the back room and sat down on a high chair behind the biggest table.

"One hundred pesetas, boys, if nobody stakes more."

Baccarat. The customers flocked to his table, the most important looking monopolizing the chairs. José was still shuffling the cards when a haggard man in mourning called out: "Banco!" and put a hundred-peseta bill on the table. He seemed to be the local gambler, for people murmured behind his back and nodded sagely when José dealt and raked in the stakes. A large-boned old man muttered behind the loser: "A bad start, Valentín."

"Just the usual thing, Uncle Juán. Anything to avoid a change."

The old man said no more, and the man called Valentín went on staking against the bank and losing. The others rarely played more than two pesetas; they were following the duel between the bank and Valentín. "The same as every night," said someone near me. People began to play against Valentín, who after an hour announced that he had used up all his cash. José asked for a continuation. The gambler protested:

"That's not fair."

"But, my dear Valentín, it isn't my fault if you've run out of cash."

"Heliodoro, give me a hundred pesetas." They went quickly.

"Heliodoro, I'll sell you my mule."

"I'll give you five hundred pesetas for her."

"Let's have them."

Heliodoro was pushing the five bank-notes along the table, when the old man who had spoken to Valentín before interposed his hand:

"Don't sell your mule, Valentín."

"I've a right to do as I like."

"All right, then, I'll give you one thousand for her."

"When? Now, at once?"

"Tomorrow morning."

"I don't need them tomorrow." Valentín took the five bills and Heliodoro scribbled a few lines on a piece of paper.

"Here, sign the receipt, Valentín."

The luck changed. Valentín heaped up bills in front of him and José had to restock the bank with cash again and again. Suddenly somebody opened the door from the street and shouted:

"Good evening!"

José gathered in the cards and his money, the others grabbed theirs, and in an instant all were sitting at the marble-topped tables and chatting boisterously. Horses' hoofs sounded on the cobbles and stopped outside the Casino. A pair of Civil Guards entered, a corporal followed by a constable.

"Good evening, gentlemen!"

José contorted himself, bowing and scraping. The Civil Guards kindly accepted a coffee each. Drinking his cup, the Corporal suddenly lifted his head and stared at me:

"You're the stranger, eh? I know already that you went to Eliseo's this afternoon." He waxed avuncular: "I'll give you some good advice — no one here will interfere with you, you can do as you like. But no meetings, eh? I want no gentlemen Communists here."

Carefully he wiped his mustache with a handkerchief, rose and walked out, followed by his silent henchman. I was dumbfounded. José sidled up to me.

"Better be careful with the Corporal, Don Arturo, he's got a foul temper."

"As long as I commit no offense, I'm no business of his."

"It's not for me to say anything, but it

isn't right for you to frequent Eliseo's. Nobody goes there except the rabble from the village, and that's God's own truth. But of course, you don't know the people yet."

Heliodoro said nothing; he listened.

The man Valentín joined us with a shining face and a fistful of bank notes.

"You've cleaned up today," said Heliodoro.

"Enough to make up for this evening, and for yesterday, and if the Guards hadn't turned up, blast them, I'd have taken the shirt off little José's back." He thumped José's plump shoulder.

"You wait till tomorrow," said José.

"Here are your six hundred pesetas, Heliodoro, and thanks."

"What's this?"

"Your six hundred pesetas."

"You don't owe me anything — well, yes, the hundred pesetas I gave you a while ago. The five hundred were for the mule."

"But d'you think I'd give you my mule for five hundred? She's worth two thousand at least!"

"You won't give her? You *have* given her. Have you sold me your mule, or not? Yes or no? Here are witnesses, and I've got your receipt in my pocket. So there's nothing more to discuss."

Valentín leaned forward:

"You son of a bitch——"

Heliodoro laid his hand on his hip pocket and smiled. He was a quiet, inconspicuous man, with taut lips.

"Look here," he said, "let's keep things straight and quiet. If you don't want to lose, don't gamble. Good night, gentlemen."

He walked off with dignity, without looking back, but a man I had not noted before stepped up, watching Valentín's every movement. Old Uncle Juán tried to steer the gambler away.

"Now, you keep quiet, and no foolishness! You've sold your mule and you can't alter it. If only it would teach you a lesson."

"But that son of a bitch——" Valentín's

eyes were watering with rage — "here's his tame gunman to cover him, too——"

José went round with a tray full of glasses of brandy.

"Now then, now then, let's have peace. After all, I've lost more than anyone."

But the game did not start again. Soon afterwards we all went out into the moonlit night. Old Juán joined me.

"We're going the same way. What do you think of our village?"

"I don't know what to say. There's food enough for thought in one day!"

"We've been discussing your visit to Eliseo's in the Casino. I think the Corporal only came to have a look at you."

"But there is no Civil Guard post in this place, is there?"

"No, they've come over from Santa Cruz. But news spreads quickly. I must say, I for one don't think it's wrong to have done what you did, and so I told the others. But if you don't take a firm stand, you'll find life difficult in our village."

"Now look here, I've no intention of getting mixed up with things in this place. After all, I'm only coming here on two days a week, and then I need a rest. But if I want to drink a glass of wine wherever I like, no one's going to prevent me."

I knew I was skirting problems, and I felt in my bones that I would not be able to skirt them for long, as I listened to the calm voice of the old man telling me a story I seemed to have heard hundreds of times, only to hate it more each time. Heliodoro was the lord and master of the township. His position as political boss was inherited from his father and grandfather who had been the usurers and *caciques*[2] of the place. Half the ground and the houses were his, and the few men who still worked their own land were dependent on him. At the coming of the Republic, people had hoped for a decent way of living. A few of the independent landowners had dared to pay higher wages. Helio-

[2] *Cacique* is the current term for the local political "boss" of the Spanish countryside, who often is the local moneylender as well. [Author's note.]

doro had proclaimed that people had to work for him at the old terms or not at all; his own living was not dependent on the land. Two years ago, the men had become desperate and destroyed trees and fields on Heliodoro's property. From that time on, he employed no labor at all, and since his latest political patrons had come to power, he gave no peace to the other proprietors.

"He fixed us with his lorries, mainly. He has got two, and so he used to carry our grain and fruit to Madrid. Most of us sold our produce direct to him. Then he refused to buy any more and our people tried to hire his lorries from him. He said no. They hired lorries in Torrijos, but because the Deputy comes from there and needs Heliodoro, the hire of the lorries was stopped. Then they hired lorries in Madrid, which was much more expensive. They had to pay double, but still, they sold their stuff in town. Then Heliodoro went to Madrid himself."

Old Juán explained how the fruit and vegetable market in Madrid was worked. A group of agents called *asentadores,* allocators, had a monopoly on the market sites. They received all produce, fixed the price according to quality and the daily market rates, and allotted the goods to the various stalls. They undertook to sell on behalf of the producer and to pay him the proceeds minus their commission.

"Well, and then, after Heliodoro's visit to Madrid, Paco, who's one of our biggest and wealthiest market gardeners, went with a lorry full of big red pimentos to market, and they were a sight for sore eyes too, and worth a lot of money. Pimentos were fetching two pesetas a dozen, and more, at that time. After three days, Paco came back from town in a fine stew and told us in the Casino what had happened to him. One after another of the allocators had told him that there was no stall available for his pimentos, and that he would have to wait. The fruit had to stay in the lorry till the evening, and then Paco had to rent storing space. Next day, the allocators told him the same old story, and said

that the market was flooded with pimentos, but they offered to take the lot off his hands at five hundred pesetas. He refused, naturally, and so another day passed. On the third day, the pimentos were squashed and dripping juice. Paco had to accept three hundred pesetas for the lot, and out of that to pay his storage, his stay at the inn, and the lorry. It was touch and go whether he would not have to pay more money out of his own pocket. When he'd finished telling the story — you can imagine in what a rage — Heliodoro laughed and said: 'You people don't understand business. No one in Novés can sell fruit in Madrid except me.' And so it was. Now, of course, people have to bring him their stuff, take what he decides to pay and dance to his tune if they want to sell anything at all. So that's why he lets his land lie fallow while the village is starving, and earns more money than he ever did from the few of us who still work. And that's why the man you saw in the Casino, and who was his father's electoral agent, has to trail round with him as his bodyguard. Because one thing is certain: Heliodoro will get it in the neck one day. Well, here you are — good night, and come and see me in my mill. It's still working."

I waited, hand on the doorknob, listening to Old Juán's footsteps dying away. They were the steps of a strong and healthy man, beautifully even. While I tried not to lose the sound, my ear was caught by the noises of the night. Frogs were croaking in the pools of the dirty stream, cicadas were shrilling tirelessly in the gully. There were little splashes and jumps, and the thin whirring sound of nocturnal insects, and the sudden creaking of old beams in some house or barn. A moon of white metal cut the street into two bands, one deep black — where I stood — and the other aggressively white, gleaming on the smooth chalk walls and glinting on the sharp flint stones. The sleeping village was beautiful in this light, but I thought I could hear the heart-beat behind the white walls, a hidden force.

My house was asleep, too. The flames in the fireplace threw huge, fugitive shadows on the walls and the two slumbering dogs were black heaps rimmed with red. I sat down between my dogs and let myself be hypnotized by the twisting flames.

The house felt empty, as I did.

The Presidential Crisis and the Split in the Socialist Party, Spring 1936

GABRIEL JACKSON

The following selection deals with the Presidential crisis of 1936, the split within the Socialist Party, and the efforts of the Republican cabinet to govern in an atmosphere of widespread ideological debate and popular unrest. It should permit the reader to judge the instability of the political situation in the months between the Popular Front victory and the outbreak of the Civil War.

The following questions are worthy of close consideration. On what grounds did the Socialist Party split between the followers of Largo Caballero and the partisans of Prieto? How do the overall issues of the spring of 1936 compare with the long-range issues discussed by Atkinson for the entire period 1898–1936? Do you find it possible to assess the relative responsibility of different classes and political groupings in the drift towards civil war?

THE ELECTION of the new President took place on May 8. The Monarchists and the CEDA officially decided to boycott the election. However, Azaña received not only the unanimous support of the Popular Front parties, but the votes of the Basque Nationalists, the *Lliga Catalana*, the handful of Lerrouxistas and Mauristas.[1] The first person to whom the new president offered the Prime Ministership was Indalecio Prieto, but the latter, in the face of the absolute opposition of the majority of the Socialist Party, declined to form a cabinet. Prieto's decision was the expression of a crisis which had been long brewing in the Socialist Party between the

moderate and the revolutionary elements.

Throughout 1934 and 1935 Largo Caballero had been talking increasingly of a Socialist revolution, while Prieto had been preaching the renewal of the Republican-Socialist coalition. At the end of 1935 the great majority of the UGT workers and the Socialist Youth favored Caballero over Prieto. Local party elections in Madrid, Murcia, and Badajoz gave overwhelming victories to the pro-Caballero slates. On December 21 *Claridad* published an analysis of the current situation and a program. The minimum program called for the nationalization of banks and land; small farmers were to be protected, but preference in distribution was to be given to collectives. The maximum program called for the dictatorship of the proletariat. Largo Caballero himself waxed sarcastic concerning

[1] The last four groups were all distinctly conservative, but in this crisis they voted for Azaña in a last effort to save the parliamentary republic as such. [Editor's note.]

From Gabriel Jackson, *The Spanish Republic and the Civil War* (Princeton, 1965), pp. 206–217. Copyright © 1965 by Princeton University Press; reprinted with the publishers' permission.

so-called socialists who feared dictatorship above all else in a world where dictatorships were becoming so frequent and successful. The editors of *Claridad* stated that the task of the moment was to consolidate the bourgeois Republic, but that inevitably the class struggle would sharpen under that regime, and that the Party must prepare for the advance to socialism.

In March, after the Popular Front electoral victory, *Claridad* published a new program. They called now for unification of the Socialist and Communist parties and the unification of the UGT and the CNT. Spain was to become a "confederation" of the Iberian peoples, including Morocco, with the right of self-determination for each people. Their phraseology had become virtually indistinguishable from that of the Communist Party organ *Mundo Obrero*. The Communists, with less than 50,000 party members and an expanding youth organization (but one which also numbered less than 50,000, in comparison with the 200,000 affiliates of the Socialist Youth) stood to gain far more than did the Socialists from any program of unification. Largo Caballero refused the Communist calls for fusion of the parties and of the UGT and CNT. He preferred to maintain the looser cooperation of the existing Popular Front. But his close adviser, Julio Alvarez del Vayo, and the most active youth leaders in Madrid such as Santiago Carrillo, Carlos de Baraibar, and the naturalized Italian Fernando de Rosa, all favored fusion. On April 1 they announced the creation of the Unified Socialist and Communist Youth (JSU), and during the spring, Rafael Vidiella, a Caballerist leader of the small Socialist unit in Barcelona, worked for the creation of the Unified Socialist-Communist Party of Catalonia (PSUC). On May Day, while Prieto at Cuenca proposed a reformist government with Socialist participation, the JSU in Madrid carried placards calling for proletarian government and the formation of a Red Army.

The young Caballerist leaders were intoxicated with the assurance that they represented "the wave of the future." They expected that in the proposed fusions they would dominate the Commmunists and educate the CNT masses to their way of thinking. They proposed to expel Besteiro from the Party on the grounds that he was not Marxist. Prieto was at best a "reformist," at worst a would-be Mussolini, planning an "Azaña-Prieto coup" to arrest the onward march of the revolution. For them, the middle class and the peasantry who had voted for the Right were not half the voters of Spain, but simply the remnant of a doomed *bourgeoisie*. They were sufficiently confident of mass support, and thus, alongside the program for socialized industry, collectivized agriculture, and a Red Army, were planks which guaranteed freedom of the press and secret suffrage. The predestined leader of the coming revolution would be the dignified, experienced, thoroughly proletarian head of the UGT, Francisco Largo Caballero. The old man himself, with a lifetime of cautious trade-union politics behind him, and mixed memories of his days in the Azaña cabinet, was both confused and flattered by the exalted terminology of *Claridad*. Somewhat to his embarrassment, and to that of the Communist Party (which at this time was seeking to reassure the *bourgeoisie*), the young Socialists began referring to Largo Caballero as "the Spanish Lenin."

During the crucial months from late 1935 into the spring of 1936, the mass of the Socialist voters looked upon Caballero as their chief. At the same time, the executive committee of the Socialist Party continued to be dominated by Prieto. In the intraparty struggle Prieto was supported strongly by the veterans of the Asturian revolt. Thousands of Socialist youth in the north had dropped their membership when the JSU was founded in Madrid. To a considerable extent, those who had seen the sufferings of the Asturian miners and villagers at close range supported Prieto, while those who had read about it supported Caballero. Prieto also enjoyed the solid support of the leading Socialist intellectuals such as Jiménez de Asúa and Juan Negrín, and that of Julián Zugazagoitia, editor of *El Socialista,* the official party organ.

In order to maintain the fragile unity of the Popular Front, Prieto had urged Manuel Azaña to accept the Presidency. Now, in the name of that same unity, he himself refused to become Prime Minister. He continued, in public speeches and in his personal newspaper, *El Liberal* of Bilbao, to denounce the infantile leftism of the UGT and CNT masses and the irresponsibility of the Caballerist leaders, who let themselves be swept along by this current. To those who insisted on interpreting the Asturian revolution as the first step toward a proletarian dictatorship, he replied that the document signed by the UGT and Socialist Party executive before the October rising had called for a program very similar to that of the present Popular Front. In October the workers had sacrificed their lives to prevent fascism. With the February electoral victory they had won a chance to effect peacefully and legally the same social program they had formulated in 1934. It was sheer madness to risk civil war for a premature revolution now.

At Cuenca and elsewhere, Prieto had been almost shouted down by hostile elements in his audience. Socialist students, sometimes accompanied by Professor Negrín, constituted an informal bodyguard on his speaking tours. On May 31 at Ecija, in the province of Seville, shots greeted him as he came out on the platform accompanied by the Asturian mine leaders González Peña and Belarmino Tomás. Just who fired the shots has never been determined. Certain Andalusian Falangists have claimed credit for the act, but their boasts must be treated skeptically. The larger truth is that in the spring of 1936 the revolutionary Socialists, the anarchists, and the Falangists would all have been fully capable of assassinating Prieto. Shortly after the Ecija incident, the Socialist Party's national convention, which had been scheduled for June, was postponed until September. The Prieto-Caballero struggle had virtually split the largest political party in Spain, and when the Party rejected Azaña's offer of a Prieto ministry, they virtually paralyzed the Popular Front government. In demanding that the Republicans govern alone, they were standing on the letter of the Popular Front pact. But everyone knew that without the Socialists, Azaña's *Izquierda Republicana* was, to use the pungent Spanish phrase, "cosa de cuatro gatos" (a matter of four cats). From *Claridad,* and from café gossip, . . . it was abundantly clear that the revolutionary Socialists assumed that by blocking an Azaña-Prieto government they were clearing the path for themselves.

The new President confided power to his faithful personal friend and political ally, Santiago Casares Quiroga. Casares had proven his ability, and his willingness to undertake difficult jobs, as Minister of the Interior during the first biennium. The landlords, the anarchists, the professional civil servants, and the various police forces under his command had all made life unpleasant for him during that period. No one knew better from personal experience how many elements of Spanish society would be happy to wreck the Republic. He was also suffering from tuberculosis and often took part in the Cortes debates while running a fever. Only through loyalty to Azaña did he consent to accept the assignment as Prime Minister on May 10, 1936.

Despite the hectic political agitation of the spring, the Republican cabinet made strong efforts to fulfill the Popular Front program. On February 29 the government suspended the eviction of agricultural tenants, a process which had been gathering momentum in late 1935. On March 16 Azaña announced once again the confiscation of the estates of the grandees involved in the Sanjurjo revolt, estates which had been confiscated in September 1932, and then restored in April 1934, as part of the

Sanjurjo amnesty law. The Minister of Agriculture, Mariano Ruiz Funes, traveled constantly in the western and southern provinces, intervening where he could to prevent clashes between the peasants and the Civil Guard and formalizing by his presence the position of thousands of squatters. The landlords cried that the government was simply legalizing robbery, but the Minister was doing the only thing that might still preserve peace in the countryside. He was pledging the government to distribute land as rapidly as possible and giving a measure of orderly procedure to actions which absolutely could not be postponed for the months that would be required to produce legislation.

In the matter of regional autonomy, the Catalan Generalitat was immediately reestablished with the powers it had exercised before October 6, and, in the course of the spring, the Madrid government transferred to it authority over public order, hydraulic works, and ports. In the Basque country the suspended municipal governments were restored, and specific discussion of a Basque autonomy statute begun. The principal difficulties to be worked out were financial. Under . . . the *concierto económico* dating back to 1878, the central government levied an agreed sum of taxes from the Basque provinces but permitted the Basques to distribute the tax burden at home as they saw fit. Articles 40 and 41 of the proposed statute guaranteed to continue this system. But in the opinion of government economic experts the Basque quota was proportionately much lower than it should have been, and the Basques of course were not ready to have the Madrid government raise their taxes. Relatively speaking, the Basques were paying smaller taxes than other Spaniards and this, together with their superior economic efficiency, tended to draw new industry to an already highly industrial area. Even Castilian liberals were not anxious to grant a statute of autonomy which would at the same time confirm a privileged position in regard to taxes.

The Popular Front pledge to restore to their jobs all workers who had been dismissed for political reasons since 1934 created serious problems. It was no easy matter to determine just who had been dismissed and for what reason. The rehiring of workers who had been fired more than a year previously inevitably meant expansion of the employer's payrolls if they were not to dismiss the more recently hired workers. Anarchist pistoleros occasionally forced employers to take on men who had never been their employees, and the general atmosphere of political tension did not ease the relationship between recent prisoners or unemployed and those who had replaced them over a period of some eighteen months. The situation was further complicated by the rivalry of UGT and CNT unions for credit in obtaining jobs for their respective clients.

In Catalonia the metal workers had won a 44-hour week shortly before the October revolt. Through 1935 they had had to work a 48-hour week without a compensating wage raise. After the February elections they demanded to be paid for all the unpaid hours of the past 15 months and turned down a Generalitat offer to compensate them by a 40-hour week at the 44-hour wage rate. The railway workers all over Spain renewed their wage demands of the years 1931–33. Railway revenues were low in 1936, as they had been in 1933. Some companies offered to show their books to prove the impossibility of meeting the demands. Many reduced their services and were glad to be taken over by the government. In Spain as in other countries the business community tolerated a measure of socialization, provided the industries taken over were those about to go bankrupt. In the spring of 1936 the Azaña and Casares governments did what they could to keep the railways in operation regardless of budgetary difficulties to be faced later.

Marcelino Domingo again was Minister of Education, as he had been in the provisional government of 1931. He restored coeducation, which had been repudiated during the second biennium, and renewed the school-building program which had come to a virtual halt in 1935. The teaching community at this time was greatly perturbed about the problem of textbooks. In the first flush of enthusiasm in 1932, the Ministry had suppressed the use of required textbooks in secondary schools. The students were to have a range of choice, and instead of taking standardized examinations, they were to submit their notebooks to the teachers. This move reflected the influence of Swiss and American progressive education in the thinking of the republicans and was also posited in part on the notion that classes would be limited to about 30 pupils. But in fact they had averaged more than 60. The teachers had clamored for the restoration of textbooks, and the conservative trend of the second biennium had favored the older methods in any case. Meanwhile, the suppression of required texts had led to the publication of many new ones. The teachers were urged to make use of the new facilities, and publishers lobbied among the Radical deputies known to be friendly to business. As a result, the students in urban high schools were forced to buy many books for the sake of a few chapters in each, and in early 1936 there were many well-substantiated complaints about profiteering in textbooks.

The clerical issue inevitably arose in connection with schools. The conservative deputies opposed coeducation and accepted with ill grace the renewal of a school-building program. However, both the Church and the government were anxious to avoid a renewal of the anticlerical passions of 1931. The Holy Week processions in Seville proceeded quietly — with extra police assigned to assure tranquility. When the temporary President, Martínez Barrio, departed for Madrid, Cardinal Ilundáin was among the dignitaries who accompanied him to the train. Using the limited information and the limited forces at its command, the government throughout the spring sent police to protect churches which the anticlericals had threatened to burn. On its side, the Church scrupulously avoided political statements of the sort made by Cardinal Segura in 1931, and the Vatican, which had not received Luis Zulueta as ambassador in 1931, accepted him promptly in 1936 when he was reappointed by Azaña. Church schools operated during the spring without interference except from occasional hooligans, but on May 20 they were ordered closed. The government claimed it was doing this to prevent the schools from being burned, an explanation which in effect admitted to a rising tide of anticlerical sentiment and to the inability of the government to control the situation. Final examinations were interrupted by the order, and Catholic parents flooded the government with letters of protest.

Prominent personalities outside the government also exerted their influence to maintain civil peace and legal forms of political action. In March, Gil Robles, explaining his electoral defeat, condemned the employers who, during the second biennium, had reduced wages vengefully. In April Manuel Giménez Fernández demanded in a caucus of the CEDA minority that the deputies take their stand for or against loyal cooperation with the Republican government. Of the 115 deputies, 101 pledged their Republican loyalty, and that 101 included those who were the personal followers of Gil Robles.

On June 2 Dr. Gregorio Marañon published a long, front-page article in *El Sol*. He deplored the exaggerated reports in the foreign press of disorders in Spain and attributed those reports to frightened reactionaries who had fled abroad after February 16 and now felt they must justify their precipitous action. He condemned the Right for having identified conservatism with the defense of every vested interest during their two years in power. He admonished the Left against the "antinational" tone of its propaganda, an indirect reference to the glorification of the Soviet Union. He warned Spaniards generally that the reforms of the Azaña government were absolutely necessary to the modernization of Spain. He predicted months of "astringent, and at times violent, friction" while this modernization proceeded, and he warned that if Azaña were defeated, all Spain would be divided between reaction and Marxism.

Miguel Maura also came forward with considered criticisms and proposals. In the June 18th issue of El Sol he began a series of articles, the best of which, concerning the Lerroux-Gil Robles governments, was unambiguously entitled Una política de suicidas. He excoriated the Right for the purely negative policy of undoing the work of the Constituent Cortes. He credited his political opponents, Azaña and Izquierda Republicana, with having saved Spain from anarchy at the end of 1935 by getting the workers to accept a Popular Front program of moderate reform. But now, five months later, Spain was suffering from an unprecedented degree of internal anarchy. "Jacobin committees" in the countryside were checkmating the best efforts of the Cortes and the civil governors. The frightened bourgeoisie were deserting their own parties [those of Gil Robles, Martínez de Velasco, Lerroux, the Lliga Catalana] and beginning to support a youthful group [the Falange] whose members were valiant and idealistic, but who lacked any precise ideal, who were wasting their energies in street battles, and who could not hope to triumph except as the result of a civil war. In view of the gravity of this situation, Maura called for a "republican dictatorship." The President should appoint a cabinet representing all tendencies from reformist socialism to conservative republicanism. That government should reestablish public order by the use of the Civil Guard, permit the highest salaries compatible with production costs and market conditions, proceed rapidly with agrarian reform, modernize the military forces, and finally, proceed to constitutional reform.

Both the gentle Dr. Marañon and the vigorous Miguel Maura were prophets without honor in the spring of 1936. Their specific proposals depended on a strengthening of the presidential power which neither the defeated Right nor the revolutionary Left would grant to Azaña. Many moderates, though they approved the Popular Front program and feared the "infantile leftism" of the young Socialists, nevertheless could not conceive a government of national union. Thus Julián Besteiro, when asked whether he would support Azaña if the latter sought CEDA votes in a struggle against a communist revolution, replied that he would never accept union with Gil Robles. Neither the Right nor the Left was in any mood to listen to the criticism offered of their general conduct. The Right, far from feeling that they had been mistaken simply to undo the work of the Constituent Cortes, felt on the contrary that they ought to have rewritten the entire document, and that if they had shot the leaders of the Asturian revolt the Popular Front would never have had the opportunity to organize. As for the Left, they were intoxicated by the notion that History was on their side. They would use the Republican government as long as it enacted the reforms they desired and then take power in the name of the proletariat, when in their eyes the time seemed ripe. They had promoted Azaña to the presidency, not to strengthen the office, but to remove from active politics the most able "bourgeois" leader. The Casares government, and any succeeding Republican government, would exist solely by grace of Socialist and Communist support in the Cortes. While the Marañons and the Mauras, the Besteiros and the Prietos, talked of ending useless strikes, stopping attacks on churches, restoring public order, the exaltados of both the Right and the Left rolled up their sleeves. When the feeble parliamentary bourgeois government had been discredited, the future would be theirs.

II. THE SPANISH CIVIL WAR AS AN INTERNATIONAL CRISIS

International Strategic Considerations and the Evolution of the Republican Government

Survey of International Affairs

The *Survey of International Affairs*, published annually by the Royal Institute, draws upon the collective services of England's finest historians and political scientists. Not infrequently it offers the best contemporary analysis available of political crises and civil wars in relation to international affairs. Two selections from the *Survey* are given below. The first deals with the strategic and geographic importance of the Spanish conflict in the perspective of several centuries of power politics. In what way is the emphasis on geographical and naval matters particularly appropriate to a British view? What evidence is given that the Spanish Civil War "was essentially a European war" being fought out in Spain? What were the international implications of the ideological factors in the Civil War?

The second selection interprets the political evolution of Republican Spain during 1938, the year in which Prime Minister Negrín tried repeatedly but unsuccessfully to obtain the support of the Western powers. What is the relationship between Negrín's program of May 1, 1938, and the international situation? To what extent could you characterize the Republican government in 1938 as revolutionary or democratic? To what degree would you consider it independent or dominated by foreign influence?

THE SITUATION OF SPAIN

IN ANOTHER CONTEXT it has been noticed that, for some two and a half centuries ending in the year 1936, the peoples of the Iberian Peninsula, with the exception of the Catalans and latterly also the Basques, had been living spiritually somewhat out of touch with the life of the modern Western World. In the same context, however, it has been noticed, besides, that this vein of spiritual aloofness had not secured for Spain an immunity from the impact of extraneous forces. In both of the two General Wars of 1672–1713 and 1792–1815 Spain had been drawn into the struggle, and Spanish territories and waters had been the scene of battles in which Spaniards as well as foreigners had been engaged. Even in the General War of 1914–18, in which Spain had preserved her neutrality, the tide of warfare had washed menacingly round her frontier, and her social fabric had been shaken by the reverberations of the struggle on the other side of the Pyrenees. In the war

From *Survey of International Affairs*, II (London, 1937), pp. 126–138; I (London, 1938), pp. 278–288. Published by Oxford University Press under the auspices of the Royal Institute of International Affairs. Reprinted by permission of the publisher.

which began in July 1936, history repeated itself with a difference. Once again, Spain was the theatre of a war in which both foreigners and Spaniards were fighting. The difference was that, instead of a general European war spreading into Spain, this time a local Spanish war threatened to extend out of Spain over Europe. This difference between the Spanish war which began in 1936 and those of 1704–13 and 1807–14 was perhaps greater in appearance than in reality; for while it was true that, down to the time of writing, the latest of these three wars, unlike its two predecessors, had been confined geographically within the frontiers of Spain, this too was essentially a European war, though it was being fought out, by tacit agreement between the principal European belligerents and neutrals, in a Peninsular arena. Nor could it even be said that these European combatants on Spanish soil had merely seized upon, and converted to their own sinister purposes, an affray that had started as a civil war between Spaniard and Spaniard. For it would have been difficult to point to an initial period, however brief, during which this war in Spain was a civil war pure and simple. The beginning of foreign intervention must be dated back at least as early as the firing of the first shot by the Nationalists; and there were indications that foreign Powers had been making preparations for the contingency of a war in Spain for some time before the actual hostilities broke out — perhaps ever since the fall of the Dictatorship of the Marqués de Estella in 1930. There was even some ground for belief that such foreign machinations had played an appreciable part in bringing the war about.

If we ask how it happened that a Spain that was so strongly inclined to hold aloof from the Western Civilization of the age was nevertheless swept, once again, into the maelström of European politics, the answer is given by the map. It was one of the tragic ironies of the Spanish people's modern history that their apparently strong desire in these latter days to make their country into something like a hermit kingdom — at least in certain departments of its life — was condemned a priori to frustration by a geographical situation which was as unchangeable as the leopard's spots or the Ethiopian's skin.

The Spain of 1936 was, of course, no longer the Spanish Empire which, at its maximum in the sixteenth century, had stretched from Sicily to the Philippines and from Friesland to Chile. The revolt of the Northern Netherlands, the encroachments of Louis XIV, the . . . transfer of Italy from a Spanish to an Austrian hegemony as a result of the War of the Spanish Succession, the secession of the continental American dominions of the Spanish Crown as a result of the Peninsular War, and finally the loss of Cuba and the Philippines in the Spanish-American War of 1898, had reduced the Spanish empire in the course of four centuries to modest dimensions. In the year 1936 Spain's possessions, outside her continental metropolitan territory in the Iberian Peninsula itself, were confined to three sets of islands — one in the Mediterranean, another in the North Atlantic, and the third in the Gulf of Guinea — and four enclaves of continental territory in Africa. Spain's Mediterranean islands were the Balearics; her Atlantic islands were the Canaries; her tropical African island was Fernando Po; her continental African possessions were the tropical enclave of Spanish Guinea, opposite Fernando Po, the two barren enclaves of Rio de Oro and Ifni, opposite the Canaries, and another strip of African territory, facing Spain herself across the Straits of Gibraltar, which was more valuable both economically and strategically. This North African strip consisted of two parts which were historically and juridically distinct. On the one hand, there were the four so-called presidios [garrisoned fortress towns] — Ceuta, Peñon de Velez de la Gomera, Alhucemas Island and Melilla — which were old and integral parts of Spain, though they happened to lie on the African side of the narrow seas.

On the other hand, there was the Spanish Zone of Morocco, which was not an ancient Spanish possession, but a Spanish protectorate of recent date. The distinction was important, because Spain's title to the occupation of this zone rested on a set of international treaties, to which France and Great Britain were parties, and which made Spain's title subject to certain conditions. She had bound herself neither to fortify this zone nor to alienate it; and the conditional character of her tenure of it had also been demonstrated *de facto* after it had been laid down *de jure*; for the effective Spanish occupation of this Spanish Zone of Morocco had only been completed with the assistance of French arms — and this as recently as the year 1926, seventeen years after the beginning of the Spanish Army's unsuccessful efforts to master the zone unaided.

It will be seen that, since the close of the sixteenth century, the Castilian Spanish Empire had shrunk in the same measure as its great contemporary, rival and counterpart the Ottoman Turkish Empire; but, by the same token, the remnant of it that survived in 1936 still occupied a geographical situation of "world-historical" importance, to use the appropriate German phrase. The Spain and the Turkey of A.D. 1936 bore, in fact, as close a resemblance to one another as the Castilian and the Ottoman Empire of A.D. 1600. In geographical terms each of these states consisted, at the later of these two dates, of a peninsula with a sea-board on each of two different seas, coupled with a bridgehead on the opposite side of a narrow waterway which was the sole maritime means of communication between one of those two seas and the other. In the Anatolian Peninsula Turkey severed the Black Sea from the Mediterranean, while in Thrace she commanded the Bosphorus, the Sea of Marmora and the Dardanelles. In the Iberian Peninsula Spain severed the Mediterranean from the Atlantic, while in North Africa (i.e. in the *presidios* in combination with the Spanish Zone of Morocco) she commanded the

Straits of Gibraltar. Another state with whose geographical position that of Spain was comparable was Denmark, with her two-fold sea-board on the Baltic and the North Sea, her half-share in the command of the Sound and the Skagerrak, and her outpost in the Faroe Islands — a Danish insular possession which was comparable, without being equal, in strategic importance to the Spanish outpost in the Canaries.

The international significance of even this much reduced Spanish Empire is manifest at a glance. In a world in which the forces of destruction were kept within bounds by the collective maintenance of a more or less effective system of international law and order, Spain, together with Turkey and Denmark, might enjoy the happiness of having no history. But in a world which was witnessing the at least temporary breakdown of that attempt at a collective organization of peace that had been made after the General War of 1914–18, the geographical situation of Spain could not fail to become a crucial factor in international affairs. For the failure — even if only for the time being — of an effort to organize a world-wide international society on a basis of justice, reason and consent re-opened the door for counter-attempts to unify the world politically by the old and evil method of the lawless abuse of superior force for the purpose of conquest and domination; and if the eclipse of the League of Nations was to be followed by an international struggle of all against all for the prize of "world power" (to use a German expression again), then it was hardly conceivable that the potential strategic importance of Spain and her possessions should not become actual.

In such a struggle the neutrality of Spain would in any case have been in jeopardy — even if the Spaniards had not facilitated foreign intervention by falling out among themselves — because of Spain's geographical bearing upon vital strategic interests of all the four European Great Powers. The balance of power between Italy and

Great Britain might be turned this way or that according to whether political control over the Spanish coasts of the Straits of Gibraltar was in hands friendly to Great Britain or at any rate neutral, or in hands friendly to Italy; and in the same way the bias of the political control over the Balearic Islands might exercise a decisive influence upon the balance of power between Italy and France. Moreover, the naval balance of power in the Mediterranean was not the only strategic question at stake; even greater issues were involved in the Spanish strategic factor in the North Atlantic.

In 1936 the Spanish Empire still debouched upon the western seaboard of the North Atlantic at four points: first, along the north and north-west coasts of the Iberian Peninsula itself, between the south-west corner of France and the north-west corner of Portugal; second, on both the European and the African flank of the Atlantic end of the Straits of Gibraltar, between the south-east corner of Portugal and the north-west corner of the French Zone of Morocco (save only for a neutral enclave cut out of the Spanish Zone of Morocco round Tangier); in the third place, in the region of the Canary Islands and the two adjoining enclaves of Spanish territory on the mainland of West Africa; in the fourth place, in the region of the Island of Fernando Po and the adjoining enclave of Spanish territory on the Guinea Coast. Of these four positions, the first was strategically the most important; for the north-west corner of Spain, Cape Finisterre, was flanked by several good harbours — Ferrol, Coruña, Vigo — and was skirted by three sea-routes of first-rate importance: the route between the Atlantic ports of France and the Atlantic ports of French Africa; the route between Great Britain and the coasts of South America from the mouth of the River Amazon to the mouth of the River Plate inclusive; and, last but not least, the "short route," via the Atlantic (as well as the "long route," via the Mediterranean), from Great Britain to South Africa, and the

"long route," round the Cape, (as well as the "short route," via the Mediterranean), from Great Britain to British East Africa, India, Burma, Malaya, Australia, New Zealand, and the Far East.

It was evident that if Italy were to obtain even an indirect control over some or all of these four Spanish frontages on the Atlantic, her ability to "make herself a nuisance" to France and Great Britain would be greatly increased; but in this Atlantic aspect of the Spanish strategic factor in international affairs Italy's interests and opportunities were not so conspicuous as Germany's. If Germany were to succeed in obtaining naval facilities at some or all of these Spanish *points d'appui* [naval bases] on the western shores of the North Atlantic, she might be in a position, in case of a conflict with the West-European Powers, to intercept the communications between France and Great Britain on the one hand and the French and British overseas empires on the other hand,[1] and at the same time she would be securing Spanish stepping-stones for her own eventual re-entry into Africa; while if she were to obtain a hold upon Spain as a whole she would gain the possibility of playing on France the trick of "encirclement" which France might be held to have been playing on Germany ever since the conclusion of the Franco-Russian alliance of 1894.

In 1936, indeed, Spain was once more the determining factor in a European balance of power. In the event of war between the "democratic" and the "Fascist" pair

---

[1] The terms of the Anglo-German naval agreement of the 18th June, 1935 had, no doubt, been offered by the German Government and accepted by the British Government as a token that Herr Hitler's Third Reich did not intend to revert to the naval policy of the Emperor William II's Second Reich, which had challenged Great Britain to an unrestricted competition in naval armaments The acquisition of naval facilities in Spanish ports might, however, enable Germany, without departing from the Anglo-German agreement of the 18th June, 1935, to incline in her own favour the resultant balance between German and British naval power — especially in view of the fact that the agreement entitled Germany to a parity with Great Britain in submarines. [Author's note.]

of European Great Powers, there would be little prospect of a decision on the continental front across which these opponents would be facing one another between the North Sea and the Atlantic. At a time when the technical advantage of the defensive over the offensive was considered by the experts to be in the order of about three to one, nothing but a military stalemate was to be expected either on the Alpine sector between France and Italy or on the Rhenish sector where the Maginot Line had presumably been matched, at the time of writing, by a German equivalent. A decision could therefore hardly be achieved unless one of the two parties could succeed in turning the other's flank; and for this purpose a command of the Iberian Peninsula would be of capital importance. If the Western Powers commanded it they might hope to succeed in establishing contact, via the Mediterranean, with the Soviet Union and any other potential allies of theirs on the eastern flank of "the Rome-Berlin Axis." On the other hand, if the Central Powers commanded the Iberian Peninsula, they might not only liberate themselves from the nightmare of a war on two fronts, but might put their Western opponents in this unpleasant quandary.

Nor were Spain's strictly strategic assets the only Spanish factors that came into consideration in the sinister play of "power politics" which had been let loose by the breakdown of the League of Nations. Spain's strategic importance was enhanced by her economic resources and by her cultural affinities.

While the economic importance of Spain and of her overseas possessions was not nearly so great as the strategic importance of the same territories in the year 1936, it was still great enough to count for something in the Spanish policy of foreign Powers. Apart from olive oil and oranges, the commodities in which Spain's production supplied an appreciable part of the world's demand were raw minerals; and while the mineral resources of Spain were rich and diverse, there were only two minerals in which her output was a dominating factor in the world's economic life. Spain at this time provided the world with some 40 to 45 per cent of its quicksilver and with more than 50 per cent of its pyrites. But the importance of particular Spanish mineral supplies could not be gauged adequately in terms of a simple proportion sum. For example, the iron ore which had been shipped, since the eighth decade of the nineteenth century, from the Three Basque Provinces and Asturias had never amounted to more than a small fraction of the world output of iron ore, and since the "peak" year 1913 the quantity exported had greatly decreased. Nevertheless, this North Spanish iron ore had a value which could not be measured in purely quantitative terms. For one thing, it was of a quality that made its use desirable, if not indispensable, for the production of the finer irons; then, again, the location of the deposits, almost at the water's edge, made it possible to ship it cheaply, especially to Great Britain; and in the third place the breakdown, since 1929, of the old system of unrestricted . . . multilateral international trade made supplies of commodities in one country important for potential consumers in other countries which were able to make favourable bilateral arrangements for reserving for their own exclusive use even supplies which amounted to no more than a small fraction of the total world supply. These considerations, of course, had special weight for countries which had consciously given up the attempt to remain participants in a world economy and had thrown themselves whole-heartedly into the contrary system of exchange-control, clearing agreements and quotas. Since Italy, Germany and Russia had all taken this road, the possibility of earmarking some of the mineral resources of Spain for their own private national use, by way of payment in kind for military and political services, was a consideration that played its part, side by side with strategic and "ideological" calculations, in the Spanish policy of each of these three Powers.

This rather summary survey of the situation of Spain cannot be closed without a glance at the cultural factor; for, on this cultural plane, what happened in Castile was likely to have repercussions in the former Spanish Empire's Latin-American successor states, while what happened in Catalonia would not be without effect either in France or in Italy. Currents of feeling circulated between Madrid and Mexico City, between Santiago de Compostella and Santiago de Chile, between Barcelona and Marseilles and Genoa. In the war which began in 1936, there were signs that, in despite of an unabated Spanish antipathy towards the modern phase of the Western form of civilization, the spiritual insulation of Spain was being broken down — partly because the modern Western World was now forcing itself upon Spain with an overwhelming violence, and partly because, as this resort to violence betrayed, the West itself at this time was reverting to the seventeenth-century spirit of which Spain had never divested herself. In the words of a letter from a distinguished Spanish philosopher-statesman, Don Salvador de Madariaga, which was published in *The Times* newspaper of London on the 19th July, 1937, and was quoted on the same day in the House of Commons at Westminster by the United Kingdom Secretary of State for Foreign Affairs, Mr. Eden,

By a tragic coincidence this war, essentially Spanish, has "caught on" abroad. Lured by somewhat shallow parallelisms, men, institutions and even Governments outside Spain have been adding fuel to the fire which is consuming our unhappy country. Spain is thus suffering vicariously the latent civil war which Europe is — so far — keeping in check.

A Transpyrenaean Liberal who at this moment found himself confronted with the prospect of a perhaps total loss of all the laboriously acquired gains of rationalism

and humanitarianism since the close of the Wars of Religion might have retorted with some sense of bitterness that the infection of a never-slaked Castilian fever seemed now to be raising to a further, and this time perhaps a deadly degree, an emotional temperature which, in the enlightened heart of the Western World, had already been rising dangerously, for the past century and a half, from the safely low point at which it had stood in the age of Leibnitz and Voltaire and Gibbon. At this critical moment the authentic accents of the Eighteenth Century could still be heard in the mouth of the French Foreign Minister. In a speech delivered at Sarlat on the 3rd August, 1936, Monsieur Delbos declared, in the name of his countrymen, that

as we do not want to risk war on any pretext, we do not want to meddle in the internal affairs of any country that you may care to name. At no price must there be a new crusade of ideals in Europe, for such a crusade would inevitably have war for its outcome.

This despairing cry of a *Weltanschauung* which, to all appearance, was now *in extremis,* received its answer on the 8th January, 1937, in an article, published in the *Osservatore Romano* [Vatican City newspaper] of that date, in which the accents of a pre-Voltairean Western Christendom made themselves heard once more:

There are several classes of intellectuals and even of statesmen who deplore the so-called war of doctrines or ideological war which, according to them, is leading Europe into a war which will be fought out not with theories but with iron. It is as well, however, to begin by clearing up a confusion of thought which lies at the root of their anxiety, namely that this war of doctrines is something peculiar to our own times, a special disease of our present civilization. In reality it is not a disease at all, not even a modern disease. It is history, it is the life of man. . . . To a militant conception of life a struggle for a doctrine is a holy war, something which, for spiritual reasons, is inevitable. Only Liberal agnosticism with its conception of tolerance in theory as well as in practice (which means the identification of truth and error and therefore scepticism), can be shocked by ideological struggles.

At this point a second confusion of thought may be denounced: that is to say the materialist conception of history, according to which, war is the affirmation of more or less selfish and material interests. . . . This materialism which calls itself historical is actually the most anti-historical of all philosophical theories of history. One may indeed say that all wars are really wars of doctrines; the conflict of ideas and the conflict of interests cannot be separated from a conflict of different conceptions of life. . . . Remember the crusades, the Christian wars against Islam, the wars of religion, French Encyclopaedism following Napoleon's armies, the Holy Alliance, even the war waged by constitutional Liberalism through half last century, the last world war for liberty and democracy, the war destined, according to Wilson, "to make the world safe for Democracy."

In A.D. 1937 it looked as though, throughout the Western World, the positive attitude that was struck in this article emanating from the Vatican City was likely to prevail over the negative attitude of the French Foreign Minister of the day; and such an event would realize Louis XIV's dream of "abolishing the Pyrenees," albeit not in the French autocrat's way. Instead of Spain's remerging herself in the general life of the Western World by surrendering at last to the comfort of a sceptical enlightenment, it now seemed not impossible that the Transpyrenaean peoples might revert to the temper of Spain by recapturing that will to pursue ideals at the price of comfort which had been condemned as "fanaticism," and eschewed as a bad bargain, by the great-grandfathers of the living generation of Englishmen and Frenchmen.

THE INTERPLAY OF NATIONALISM AND IDEOLOGY

The vehemence of the passions which the war in Spain excited in the Transpyrenaean countries was perhaps more remarkable in France and Great Britain

than elsewhere, because these two countries had been, for the past two and a half centuries, the very hearth and home of the prosaic, anti-Quixotic philosophy of life that was the "pre-totalitarian" form of a modern Western paganism. It was the creed of this Liberal philosophy that Folly became indistinguishable from Crime when she took up arms in vindication of interests that were not utilitarian; and therefore the spectacle of a France and an England convulsed by ideological passions looked like a portent of the end of an epoch. In the same year, 1936, the same passions were also aflame in the three great "totalitarian" countries of Central and Eastern Europe; but the situation in Italy, Germany and the Soviet Union differed from that in Great Britain and France in one respect that was fraught with important practical consequences.

In each of the "totalitarian" countries there was a twofold resolution of forces which, on a short view, endowed all these countries with a formidable *Aktionsfähigkeit* [capability of action] in a struggle for "world power," though on a longer reckoning this immediate politico-military advantage might have to be paid for at the price of spiritual impoverishment and even bankruptcy. In the first place the "totalitarian" régimes were, by definition, intolerant, as far as their effective authority extended, of any "ideologies" that conflicted with their own; and in all these countries alike the expression in speech or writing, and *a fortiori* the translation into action, of any creed contrary to that of the party in power had been suppressed by brute force. In each of these countries one voice only was now heard because all other voices had been either muffled in the concentration camp or smothered in the grave. There was no confusion of counsels, because there was no debate; and this first short-term advantage was reinforced by a second. In each of these three countries the unchallenged will of the ruling phalanx was in harmony with *raison d'état* as this would have been conceived by an eighteenth-century adept in the art of statesmanship. An Italian Fascist and a German National Socialist and a Russian Communist could enjoy the exhilaration of feeling that in serving his party he was serving his country too, while conversely a patriotic German or Italian or Russian who was indifferent, or even hostile, to the reigning régime and to its intolerant "ideology" could still enjoy the consolation of feeling that a régime for which he could have no enthusiasm in any other regard was at any rate working in the common national cause as energetically and as successfully as the patriotic critic himself could desire.

These two points of immediate strength in the Soviet Union, Germany and Italy were unequally matched in France and Great Britain by two corresponding points of immediate weakness. In the first place, conflicting "ideologies" were allowed, *ex hypothesi*, in countries which prided themselves on being democratic and which jealously treasured their traditional domestic liberties, to contend with one another without fear or favour, even to the point of confusing counsels and impeding action. The French and British Governments of the day could not silence the Opposition without being guilty of a revolutionary abuse of their constitutional powers. For such an imitation of "totalitarian" politics the parliamentarian-minded French and British politicians then in office had no stomach. In so far as they were faced with a choice between unlawfully muzzling the Opposition and inexpediently allowing themselves to be handicapped by it, they unhesitatingly and steadily preferred the latter of these two evils. The Opposition's sacrosanct power to obstruct the policy of the Government in office did not, however, at this time carry with it the logically complementary power to turn the Government out and take office themselves for the purpose of attempting some different policy of their own. The consequence of this mutual frustration of Opposition and Government was a feebleness, which in crises often verged upon paralysis, in the

conduct of French and British foreign policy. And this weakness was aggravated by the further misfortune that the policy which was demanded of the French and British Governments at this time by considerations of *raison d'état* was on the whole perhaps more in consonance with the "ideology" of a party which, in the sphere of foreign affairs, was virtually, even if not technically, in opposition than with that of the party in accordance with whose views and wishes the Government's policy was being shaped.[2] Thus in the "democratic" countries there was a double conflict — on the one hand between the respective "ideologies" of the Opposition and the Government, and on the other hand between that "ideology" with which the Government — or the governing elements in the body politic — were in sympathy and the dictates of *raison d'état* as these might have presented themselves if the interest of the country had been disengaged from all "ideological" considerations and had been pursued with a "totalitarian" single-mindedness.

This twofold political paralysis co-operated with a moral aversion from, and a material unreadiness for, war to render the two West European "democratic" Powers at least temporarily incompetent, by comparison with their "totalitarian" neighbours, for taking effective action in a forum that was now threatening to degenerate into an arena. It was true that the "totalitarian" Governments were hardly less anxious (as far as could be judged) than the "democratic" Governments were to avoid "major"

[2] This was manifest in Great Britain under the so-called "National Government"; but the situation was fundamentally the same in France under the administration of Governments representing the so-called "Front Populaire"; for in their foreign policy MM. Blum and Chautemps, no less than Messrs. Baldwin and Chamberlain, were to a large extent carrying out the ideas and desires of the Right, while conversely the French Socialists and Communists were as strongly opposed to this foreign policy that was professedly being carried out in their name as the British Labour Party were to the foreign policy that was admittedly being carried out in their despite. [Author's note.]

wars with Powers of their own calibre. They were, however, prepared — to an extent that was revealed by the lengths to which they went in Spain in violating the Non-Intervention Agreement — to incur greater risks of war for the sake of pursuing their national ambitions than the "democratic" Governments were ready to incur for the sake of defending their national interests. In situations in which an eighteenth-century, or even a nineteenth-century, French or British Government might have preferred to accept a risk of war to-day rather than postpone that risk to a morrow on which it might have to be accepted, after all, under more adverse conditions, the "democratic" French and British Governments of the years 1936–7 showed themselves determined to abstain from any action that might involve a risk of war forthwith, and this even in cases where it was probable that such abstention would give away formidable potential advantages to Powers who would almost certainly be in the opposite camp if another general war did break out later notwithstanding all the efforts of French and British diplomacy. They were not only unwilling to use war themselves as an instrument of national policy; they were unwilling even to exercise their legitimate rights in the sphere of non-military action if there was a risk that the exercise of them might move other Powers to take illegitimate military reprisals. In thus doing their best to make sure of peace to-day, the two Governments were, to all appearances, carrying out the wishes of a majority of the people in either country, however loudly the opposing voices might protest. And when this hazarding of long-term national interests, including perhaps the ultimate preservation of peace itself, worked out in harmony with the "ideological" proclivities of some at least of the politicians who had to take the decisions, the choice for the Governments in London and Paris was as heavily weighted in favour of inaction as the choice for the Governments in Berlin, Rome and Moscow was weighted

in favour of action *sub rosa*. The three "totalitarian" Powers were, indeed, assiduous in breaking their non-intervention engagements to the two "democratic" Powers up to the extreme limit of French and British forebearance; and the unwillingness of the two Western Powers to follow suit in this deplorable game put them at a further disadvantage which did them no dishonour. The whole policy of non-intervention, as proposed by the "democratic" Powers and nominally accepted by the "totalitarian" Powers, presupposed the maintenance of a certain traditional standard of honesty in diplomatic dealings; and the "democratic" Powers made no unreasonable demand in expecting of their neighbours a modicum of straightforwardness, short of which it was difficult to see how any kind of international intercourse could continue.

*   *   *

POLITICAL DEVELOPMENTS IN REPUBLICAN SPAIN

At the beginning of 1938 Republican Spain was still being governed by the coalition of Socialists, Communists and the more moderate Republican parties, including Basque and Catalan regionalists, which had come into office in May 1937 with Dr. Negrín as Premier and Señor Prieto as Minister of Defence. The right-wing Socialists and moderate Republicans were, perhaps, the strongest element in the coalition, but a bid for ascendancy was also being made by the Communists. These claimed to be the firmest defenders of national independence, of the Republican constitution, and of the liberties of the peasants, workers and small bourgeoisie, but, however emphatically they might protest to the contrary, there was also reason to believe that they meant to rule the country after the war without any compromise with other parties. Their tendency towards party dictatorship and police terrorism, and their frequently unscrupulous methods of penetrating into or absorbing other organizations made them enemies even among those Republicans who would otherwise have agreed with their moderate, not to say anti-revolutionary, . . . economic policy and their insistence on discipline and efficiency. On the other hand, their supporters and sympathizers in the army included Lister, Modesto, El Campesino and others of the best-known Republican commanders. They were particularly anxious to extend their influence here, as they believed that the army would be the real ruler of Spain in the event of a Republican victory. With this end in view they had worked for the replacement of Señor Largo Caballero by Señor Prieto only to find that the new Minister of Defence was no less determined than his predecessor to prevent them from growing too powerful. Steps had recently been taken to restrict the activities of the political Commissars, many of whom had acted as missionaries of Communism, and a number of non-Communist officers, who had held commissions before the outbreak of the war, had been appointed to high positions in the army. The Communists replied with threats that if there were not enough political Commissars there would be no more Russian aeroplanes.

Moscow Communism had even less influence over the Popular Front groups which still remained outside the Government. Loyalty to Marxism did not prevent left-wing Socialists from saying that they would fight Comintern interference as fiercely as they were fighting Fascism; and the Anarcho-Syndicalists of the Federación Anarquista Ibérica and the Confederación Nacional del Trabajo had Communist doctrines of their own which had no direct connexion either with Marx or with Stalin's Moscow. The difference between the "libertarian" Anarchists and the "authoritarian" Stalinite Communists was one of the most striking contrasts of the civil war, and, even in the early days of Anarcho-Syndicalism, the foreign revolutionaries who had introduced it into Spain had been followers not of Marx but of Bakunin. In any case the ideological pedigree of Anarcho-Syndicalism is less important than the immediate response which it had aroused from the Spanish proletariat, long before Marxist Communism had triumphed in Russia. It was only natural that it should have had a special attraction for Spaniards, who have been described by a brilliant critic of their own race as "a profoundly individualistic people, usually passive" but at the same time capable of "volcanic eruptions of energy," a people full of contradictory qualities in whom great generosity could be found side by side with fierce envy, messianic hopes for the future and an utter indifference to pain. It was these national characteristics that were the driving force behind Anarcho-Syndicalism and the other extremist movements in Spain, and that were the real cause of the murders and church-burnings and wild economic experiments. To illustrate this point one might compare Spain with one of the geysers in the Yellowstone Park which can be artificially stimulated into spouting up their hot water and steam for the benefit of tourists. Moscow as well as the Axis Powers may have helped to put soap down the geyser's mouth, but the explosive forces below were purely Spanish, and the banishment of Marxism from Spain would not prevent violent eruptions happening in future without the help of any outside interference.

Extreme though the views of the Anarcho-Syndicalist leaders were, they had somewhat modified them during the war. In spite of their objections to political action they had, for instance, been represented in Señor Largo Caballero's Government until its fall in May 1937, and in the spring of 1938 they wished to return to office. Some of the Republican leaders were willing to agree to this, but others feared that the change would be too alarming to public opinion in the western countries. The reconstruction of Dr. Negrín's Government which took place on the 5th April was a consequence of the Nationalist successes in Aragon and was more to the advantage of the Communists than to that of the Anarcho-Syndicalists. Dr. Negrín himself now took the post of Minister of Defence in place of Señor Prieto, who had been held responsible for the recent defeats. Señor Prieto, who had been held responsible for the recent defeats. Señor González Peña of the Socialist trade unions became Minister for Justice, Señor Gomez Sainz of the Socialist Party, who had lately been in control of public order in Catalonia, became Minister for the Interior, and Señor Álvarez del Vayo returned to his former post of Minister for Foreign Affairs. The Basques, Catalans and Republican Union and Republican Left parties took part in this Government as they had done in the last. A representative of the Confederación Nacional del Trabajo was appointed to the Ministry of Health and Education, but, whereas the Communists had now apparently only one representative (at the Ministry of Agriculture) instead of two, they had in reality gained a valuable ally in Señor Álvarez del Vayo. The new Government soon decided to allow greater scope to the political commissars, and shortly afterwards Señor Hernández, the outgoing Communist Minister for Education, was made chief War Commissar for the separated territories of Central and Southern Spain. Communist influence in the General Staff was also increased by the appointment of Colonel Modesto in place of General Rojo.

The policy of the new Government was expounded by Dr. Negrín on the 1st May in a thirteen-point declaration, the chief items of which may be summed up as follows:

The maintenance of the independence and integrity of Spain and its deliverance from invasion and economic penetration; the determination of the legal and social form of the new Republic by the national will expressed in a free plebiscite with full guarantees against reprisals, which would be held as soon as hostilities were at an end; respect for regional liberties, in accordance with law and historical tradition, in so far as these liberties did not impair the unity and integrity of Spain; a guarantee by the state to all citizens of "full civil and social rights, including freedom of conscience," and an assurance of "the free exercise of religious beliefs"; guarantee by the state of the right to hold lawfully acquired property, within limits determined by the supreme interests of the nation; exploitation would be prevented, but individual enterprise would be allowed and small property-owners would be encouraged, the property of foreigners who had not assisted the Nationalists would be respected, and compensation would be paid for damage done to it as a result of the war; agrarian reform and the creation of a rural democracy owning the land that it worked; adoption of a foreign policy renouncing war, supporting the League of Nations and collective security, and claiming a place for Spain in the Concert of Nations as a Mediterranean Power fully capable of defending herself; an amnesty for all Spaniards willing to take part in the reconstruction and liberation of their country.

Promises similar to these thirteen points had often before been made by Republican leaders. To take examples from the first three months of 1938, Dr. Negrín's speech to the Cortes at their session of the 1st February promised that the Government would restore constitutional administration as soon as war conditions permitted, and declared that they had no desire to exterminate their opponents; and his broadcast speech of the 28th March appealed to intellectuals, small industrialists and the Catalan middle class to unite in defending Spain against invaders who were foreigners as well as Fascists. This appeal for union against the foreign enemy had, of course, its counterpart in Nationalist Spain, where Russians, French and Czechs replaced Italians and Germans as the villains of the piece. In Republican Spain, however, this appeal continued to be accompanied by the promises of reconciliation and the restoration of civil and regional liberties. President Azaña, speaking at Barcelona on the 18th July, made the plea that "we are all fellow countrymen, even the conquered." A month earlier Dr. Negrín, speaking at Madrid on the 18th June, had declared that "not one second more of war" could be endured if "the existence of Spain as a free country" was not at stake. He also expressed the hope that, "before many years had gone by, the names of all the victims of the struggle would appear side by side on the war memorial of each village." And he asserted that, though the Church must no longer interfere in politics, the guaranteeing of free religious worship was a duty which the Republican Government owed to their own liberal principles, as well as to the thousands of loyal Catholic citizens. He added that without deep religious feeling it would be difficult to endure the ordeal to which Spain was being subjected.

The thirteen points very probably echoed a genuine desire on the part of some at least of the Republicans for reconstruction without reprisals, anti-religious intolerance or a return to violent social revolution. On the other hand, Republicans who were not Communists suspected that this was to some extent another case of Communists trying to outdo the moderates in moderation. It was also true that declarations of this kind had an obvious value as appeals to the sympathy of the "democratic" nations at a time when the Republicans were hard pressed by the advance of the Nationalists in the field of battle and by their own economic difficulties behind the lines.

The prospects of a successful reconstruction of Spain on the basis of these points, if the Republicans had won the war, can only be judged by studying those political and other developments during the year which show how far the Republican Government were masters in their own house; and how they dealt with such problems as economic organization, the maintenance of order and the toleration or persecution of the Roman Catholic Church.

As regards the stability of Dr. Negrín's Government, it may be noted that they remained in office until after the military collapse of Catalonia in January 1939.

Nevertheless the change of Cabinet had not put an end to party dissensions, particularly between Communists and non-Communists. These dissensions did much to weaken Republican efficiency and will to resist and were among the main causes of their defeat. The strongest opposition which the Negrín Government had to face did not now come from extremists but from moderates who could not accept the policy of a fight to a finish. President Azaña was already believed to be in favour of obtaining a truce as soon as possible, on condition that it should be followed by a plebiscite. Another Republican leader who seems all along to have been unwilling to continue the war to the bitter end was Señor Besteiro, a right-wing Socialist; and it had been hinted that he or Señor Martínez Barrio might some day help to form a Government of Reconciliation. Many of the Catalan bourgeoisie were in favour of an early truce, and Catalan opinion also tended to dislike the way in which the Republican Government were encroaching on Catalonia's constitutionally established autonomy. The maintenance of order in Catalonia had been in the hands of the Republican Government since May 1937, and since the beginning of the year they had taken control of the supply of food and had been attempting to replace the collectivization of industry by state supervision. The Generalitat also complained that they had to finance the public services which remained under their control without receiving any share of the benefits derived by the Republican Government from currency inflation or foreign trade. High officials of the Generalitat seem, however, still to have been hoping that, after a Republican victory, the Catalans might be granted even wider concessions than those originally provided by the Statute of 1932. On the other hand, any doubts with regard to the Nationalist attitude towards Catalan self-government had been cleared up by the Burgos decree of the 5th April annulling the Statute altogether.

The first crisis which the Government

surmounted during the summer came to a head in June and seems to have been connected with allegations that certain Republican leaders had gone abroad to open negotiations with regard to the foreign policy of the Republic and the outcome of the war. No change was, however, made in the Government until the middle of August, after the questions of regional liberties and revolutionary justice, as well as the underlying division of opinion on the issue of resistance or surrender, had been raised by the introduction of decrees placing the Catalan ports and war industries under military discipline and under the control of the Central Republican Government, and establishing a special tribunal in Catalonia to judge cases arising out of the flight of capital. Señor Irujo, a Basque Nationalist who was at that time Minister without Portfolio, joined with the Minister for Labour, a member of the Catalan party called the Esquerra to oppose these decrees, and the whole Government resigned on the 16th August. Special precautions were taken and many arrests were made, but the crisis passed off without any of the disturbances that had been feared. Next day the two recalcitrant Ministers were replaced by Basque and Catalan Socialists.

The position with regard to the maintenance of law and order may be summed up as follows. There were no signs during 1938 of a return to the violent state of revolution, which had worked itself out and had been brought under control in the course of 1937. For instance, an English journalist who spent a fortnight or more in and near Teruel while the Republicans were occupying it, only came across five cases of shooting prisoners out of hand. The terrorism which had been carried on by gangsters and "uncontrolled revolutionaries" was now practically at an end, and an account of the situation at Madrid in the early months of the year could state that it was "many months since corpses" had "littered the outskirts" of that city. In Barcelona, also, this kind of terrorism had greatly decreased. With the strength-ening of the authority of the Republican Government, and the growth of Communist influence, however, police terrorism and the persecution of Republicans considered as heretics by a stronger faction had increased. The Government had taken action against the detachments of the Russian G.P.U. who had been in control of the Communists' private courts and police force, but the Socialist Minister of the Interior had set up a "Cheka" of his own in December 1937 in the shape of a council for the defence of the régime which was free from any judiciary control. Señor Irujo, the Basque Minister of Justice, had shown his disapproval of this proposal by resigning. The actual work of hunting out spies and traitors was done by an organization called the Servicio de Investigación Militar which soon became very powerful. This, too, was under Communist influence and was managed by the official Spanish political police, who had the knack of surviving any revolution. In March 1938, at the time of the Nationalist break-through in Aragon, special summary tribunals were established to deal with cases of spying, treason and defeatism, with which came to be included profiteering, food-hoarding and armed robbery. During the following month, when it seemed possible that Catalonia might shortly be invaded by the Nationalist armies with the help of risings by Nationalist sympathizers behind the lines, it was perhaps not unnatural that a specially large number of suspects should be rounded up in Barcelona. It was at this time, too, that members of the S.I.M., apparently without the knowledge of their superior officers, began a murder campaign of their own. Twenty or thirty people had been "taken for a ride" before the judges of Barcelona succeeded in putting pressure on the Government to bring the S.I.M. to heel.

The more regular activities of the S.I.M., however, continued to bear fruit during the rest of the year in the shape of trials for various crimes affecting the safety of the régime. A number of high military and civil officials were among the accused, and many people were sentenced to death. In August 1938, however, the Republican Government had tried to prepare the way for a general amnesty by proposing that each side should suspend the execution of death sentences on military prisoners for a month; and though no agreement was reached on this point, both Nationalists and Republicans seem to have considerably reduced the number of executions of civil as well as military prisoners during the rest of the year.

One of the most important trials which took place in Republican Spain during the autumn was that of seven leaders of the anti-Stalinite Communist party called the Partido Obrero de Unificación Marxista. Though the Stalinite Communists had for long been insisting that the P.O.U.M. leaders had been acting as spies for the Nationalists, all charges of this kind against them were dropped on the ground of insufficient evidence, and though five of the prisoners were found guilty of taking part in rebellion during the Barcelona disturbances of May 1937, they did at least escape the death sentence. The Russian Government were said to have been much displeased that the Republicans had deprived them of a chance to justify their own "purges" by proving, by hook or by crook, a connexion between Trotskyism and Fascism in Spain.

The treatment of prisoners seems to have varied a good deal. In Barcelona the worst conditions were to be found in the special prisons of the S.I.M., about which unpleasant revelations were made after the fall of Barcelona, and in the three ships which were kept full of prisoners until October 1938, and which were also in continual danger of being bombed, though, as it happened, they were never actually hit. On the other hand an English press correspondent was told by the relatives of people who had been sent to the new Model Prison that conditions there were good and that political prisoners were treated with consideration. The same correspondent reported that "noisy political discussions" could "often be heard" in cafés or on railway trains in which the Government were "openly criticized and condemned." "Considerable hardship" was, however, "suffered by persons who, owing to associations or actions before the war," were "now under suspicion."

"The free exercise of religious beliefs" mentioned in Dr. Negrín's sixth point was far from being completely restored during the year. There was no general reopening of churches, and Catholic worship was allowed to be performed only in private houses by priests licensed by the Government. Permission was never even given to open the French chapel in Barcelona. The Basques, who were allowed to hold services in their own regional government offices, were constantly urging that greater freedom should be given, but the Republican Government were not yet willing to carry out their promises of toleration, alleging that public opinion was still too hostile. In Barcelona, where the attack on religion had been fiercest, about a quarter of the priests had been killed early in the revolution, but some of those who had escaped abroad had since returned, and nearly 2,000, or at the most 2,500, were believed to be living there in the spring of 1938. These priests had to go about dressed as laymen and were liable to be accused of belonging to the "fifth column." More than one was sentenced to death during the year on the charge of taking a leading part in Nationalist conspiracies.

The concessions and conciliatory gestures which were made in the course of the year were very small and influenced, to a great extent, by the needs of political manœuvring at home and of propaganda abroad. From March 1938 onwards, priests who were called up for military service were drafted into the medical corps, and it was understood that they would be allowed to minister to the souls as well as the bodies of their patients; a decree issued on the 26th June ordered all commanding officers of the armed forces to allow any of their men to have access to a minister of their religion; and, both on the Madrid and Ebro fronts, soldiers were reported to have been attending Mass. The strong Communist influence in the army might not be unfavourable to these changes being carried out, since the Communists now maintained that their quarrel was not against religion, but only against the economic and political power of the Church. It was perfectly in keeping with the opportunism of the Stalin period for Communists to make a bid for the friendship of the Roman Catholic Church just as they were bidding for the support of the middle class. It did not necessarily follow that the Church would respond to those advances or that Catholics would receive better treatment in a Communist-ruled Spain than in other Communist or National-Socialist states. The most dramatic of the Government's friendly gestures was the public funeral procession in honour of a Basque officer killed on the Ebro front which passed through the streets of Barcelona on the 17th October, with full religious ceremonial and with Señor Álvarez de Vayo and many army officers among the mourners. A move by the Government which there was less reason to suspect of being staged for foreign beholders was the decree of the 9th December providing for the setting up of a Commissariat General of Religion, but the Republican régime did not survive long enough to show what the effect of this would have been.

In economic affairs, one of the Republican Government's chief difficulties was still that they had at one and the same time to cope with a civil war and with a social revolution. When they wished to make up for the loss of food-producing provinces, or for the blockade and the non-intervention agreement, by growing more food and producing more war material in their own territory, they found that the economic system had become a battlefield where trade unions and other Republican groups were firmly entrenched in positions which they had captured on their own initiative. For instance, all the transport services in Catalonia were still being managed "collectively," that is to say by committees of workers, and the lack of cooperation between these committees and the municipalities greatly hindered the distribution of supplies. By the beginning of 1938, however, the Republican Government were trying to replace collectivization by state control. They were now appointing "interveners" to act as managers of factories and businesses and to choose boards of directors including the former owners, if still available, as well as workers' representatives. The Department of Economy would then provide these businesses with raw materials and market the goods which they produced. Many of the workers were now said to have wanted to give up collectivization, and attempts were made, but with little success, to persuade business men to return to Republican Spain. The retreat from the revolution was, in any case, a slow process, and it was easier to apply it to small firms than to give the Catalan war industries the reorganization of which they were so badly in need.

The Nonintervention Committee and Italo-German Aid to the Nationalists

DANTE PUZZO

The following selection by Professor Puzzo, of the City College of New York, treats in some detail the beginnings of the nonintervention agreement. In noting the activities of the several ambassadors and foreign secretaries, the author emphasizes the pathetic optimism of the French, and the several reservations which Portugal, Italy, and Germany attached to their original adherence.

It is a fact also that the "agreement" was really just a series of unilateral declarations of intent, and it included no binding legal clauses and no machinery for enforcement. In its operation the agreement effectively prevented the Spanish Republican government from buying arms in Europe or America, while it never in any way inhibited the fascist powers from arming the Nationalists, nor the Soviets from arming the Republicans. Nevertheless, since the material quoted below highlights so strongly the failure of nonintervention, there are several questions which the reader should consider very carefully. Why did many democratic governments, including that of the United States, support the nonintervention agreement? What were the precise reservations attached by Italy, Germany, and Portugal to their original adherence? Were these reservations of such a nature as to cripple the agreements in advance? If there had been no agreement at all, might the Civil War have escalated into a world war in 1937?

THE MONTH OF AUGUST, 1936, saw twenty-seven European nations formally adhere to the nonintervention agreement. However, this did not mean that by the end of that eventful summer foreign interference in the Spanish conflict had ceased, or even had appreciably diminished. On the contrary, the evidence is incontrovertible that foreign intervention in Spain was considerably greater and more open following the general agreement not to intervene than it had been before. If the flow of war supplies from France to Republican Spain was reduced to a mere trickle, then that from Germany, Italy, and Portugal to the Spanish rebels became a torrent. Moreover, before the cold winds of winter blew out of the Sierra de Guadarrama across the Castilian plain, thousands of volunteers from all parts of the earth had flocked to Madrid to form the International Brigades. Meanwhile, from places as distant as Mexico and Soviet Russia came arms, munitions, and supplies for the embattled Republic. The help that Soviet Russia sent was to grow both in volume and importance. This sequence of events had been adumbrated in the exchange of notes, in the proposals and counter-proposals, in the procrastination and legalistic artifices which marked the diplomacy that had resulted in the formal adherence of the European powers to the nonintervention agreement.

Following initial overtures to Great Britain and Italy concerning an agreement not to intervene in the Spanish conflict, the French government addressed similar appeals to Germany, Portugal, and Soviet Russia. On August 4, 1936, the British gov-

From Dante A. Puzzo, *Spain and the Great Powers 1936–1941* (New York, 1962), pp. 104–109, 111–120, 125–126. Reprinted by permission of Columbia University Press.

ernment replied that it agreed in principle with a policy of nonintervention in Spanish affairs. However, on August 6, the Italian foreign minister, Count Galeazzo Ciano, informed both the French Ambassador and the British Chargé d'Affaires in Rome, who, in support of his French colleague, had handed Ciano an *aide-mémoire* relating to the French proposal for a nonintervention agreement and indicating Great Britain's acceptance in principle, that while Italy also agreed in principle with a policy of nonintervention the Italian government was greatly concerned with "ideological and spiritual" intervention in Spain which "must be prevented at the same time as, and concurrently with, the supply of arms." Ciano's reference to "ideological and spiritual" intervention was, of course, a reference to the activities in support of the Spanish Republic by private organizations and private individuals in England, France, and Soviet Russia (in this last instance the "private" character of such activity was open to legitimate doubt). The Ciano-Chambrun talks floundered on this reef for the next few days. Then, on August 14, the French Ambassador informed the Italian Foreign Minister that the French government agreed in principle with the Italian proposal to prevent the subscription of funds and the recruitment of volunteers for Spain. However, Chambrun expressed the concern of the French government that the Italian proposal might result in further delay in the conclusion of a general agreement and suggested that in order to expedite the matter the French conception of the nonintervention agreement be submitted to the other powers but with the Italian suggestions duly noted. Ciano replied that this "appeared absolutely unacceptable" but that he would discuss the Ambassador's proposal with the Duce. There the matter stood for the next few days.

Meanwhile, the French ambassador in Berlin, André François-Poncet, was experiencing the same frustration with the German foreign minister, Baron Constantin von Neurath. As was noted, the French Ambassador first broached the idea of a nonintervention agreement to the German Foreign Minister on August 4, 1936, only to be informed that Germany "naturally did not intervene in Spanish internal political affairs and disputes." However, Baron von Neurath indicated that Germany was prepared "to participate in a discussion aimed at preventing the extension of the Spanish Civil War to Europe" but only if all the interested powers, particularly Soviet Russia, adhered to the nonintervention agreement that might result from such a discussion. On August 7 François-Poncet again called on Baron von Neurath and handed him a draft of the French declaration of nonintervention in Spain. The German Foreign Minister promised to study the draft "thoroughly" but forthwith noted the great difficulties which would attend the enforcement of the French scheme. Baron von Neurath stressed that these would be particularly onerous with respect to the activities of the Comintern which, the official attitude of the Soviet government notwithstanding (François-Poncet had informed Baron von Neurath that Moscow had agreed in principle to a policy of nonintervention), would not be bound by it. François-Poncet conceded that the difficulties attendant upon the enforcement of the nonintervention agreement would be great but insisted that agreement by the principal states of Europe on an arms embargo would constitute an excellent beginning.

The following day, August 8, the British ambassador in Berlin, Sir Eric Phipps, called at the German Foreign Ministry and expressed his "warmest support" of the French proposal concerning nonintervention in Spain. Baron von Neurath assured his British visitor that the German government was "carefully examining" its reply. Then the Baron called the attention of Sir Eric Phipps, as he had that of M. François-Poncet, to the practical difficulties of such a plan and suggested that in order to be truly efficacious it would have to include all countries with "a large arms and munitions industry of their own" and, therefore, the United States, Sweden, and Switzerland. The Baron, moreover, expressed his doubts concerning the sincerity of the Russians.

To insist that all countries with "a large arms and munitions industry of their own" be included in the nonintervention scheme was patently dilatory on the part of the German government. To specifically mention the United States, Sweden, and Switzerland was particularly gauche on the part of Baron von Neurath. For Sir Eric Phipps must have been aware that Berlin was not unaware that the American Republic, which had refused to join the League of Nations and in which isolationist sentiment continued widely manifest, could hardly be expected to adhere formally to the nonintervention agreement and that Sweden and Switzerland were "traditionally neutral states."

The misadventure of a German pilot provided the German government with further occasion to continue its dilatory tactics. On August 9, 1936, the pilot of a German tri-motor Junkers 52, the D-AMIM, landed at the Madrid airport but, perceiving that he had made a mistake, immediately took off again to come down later at Badajoz. However, on August 9 Badajoz was still held by Republican forces. The German aircraft was impounded and its crew interned. When the German government learned of the incident, it instructed its chargé d'affaires in Madrid, Hans Voelckers, to demand that the Spanish government order the immediate release of the airplane and its crew. The Spanish government refused to comply on the ground that inasmuch as the airplane had been flown over Spanish territory without proper authorization it was necessary for the Spanish government to make a thorough investigation of the incident. Acting on instructions from Baron von Neurath, Dr. Karl Dumont, head of Political Division III of the German Foreign Ministry, telephoned the French am-

bassador in Berlin on August 12 and informed him that the German government was prepared to agree in principle to a policy of nonintervention in Spain but could not do so as long as the Spanish government continued to hold the German aircraft and its crew. On August 13, the German chargé d'affaires in Madrid handed the Spanish foreign minister, Señor Augusto Barcia, a note in which the German government again demanded the immediate release of the D-AMIM and its crew and which warned that "should the government of the Spanish Republic fail to comply with this justified demand, the German government would feel obliged to resort to the most serious measures." In its quarrel with Madrid, Berlin found support in Paris. On August 15 the French Government, hoping to remove the last obstacle to German adherence to the nonintervention plan, urged the Spanish government to comply with the German demand. But Madrid, possibly out of a desire not to see the nonintervention agreement consummated, proved obstinate. It consented to release the crew of the D-AMIM but continued to hold the aircraft itself. There the matter stood for the next few days.

Meanwhile, on August 7, both the British and French governments had invited Portugal to adhere to the nonintervention plan. The Portuguese foreign minister, Dr. Armindo Monteiro, while promising to give "careful consideration to this invitation," had noted the "special dangers for Portugal arising from the present situation in Spain" and had intimated that Portugal in its own defense might find it necessary to recognize and assist the Burgos government, i.e., the Spanish rebels. On August 13, however, Lisbon had informed London and Paris that the Portuguese government agreed in principle with a policy of nonintervention in Spain but that it reserved "liberty of action in case an emergency arises involving the security of Portuguese frontiers or the internal peace and security of Portugal itself."

It can be assumed that this *volte-face* on

the part of the Portuguese government resulted, in large measure at least, from British diplomatic pressure. However, Lisbon's agreement in principle to nonintervention in Spain was little more than a gesture, for Portugal continued to abet materially the rebel cause and Portuguese newspapers, including those of a semiofficial character, greeted the fall of Badajoz with headlines to the effect that "Portugal has now ceased to have any frontier with robbers and assassins." . . .

On August 15, 1936, the French government, without waiting for general agreement on the matter but hoping thus to expedite it, issued a formal declaration of nonintervention in the Spanish struggle. This declaration was in the form of a note addressed by the French foreign minister, Yvon Delbos, to the British ambassador in Paris, Sir George Clerk. It was to become the prototype of similar declarations by the majority of the other powers which ultimately adhered to the nonintervention agreement, including those of both Great Britain and Soviet Russia. The French declaration follows:

Paris, August 15, 1936

Mr. Ambassador,

The negotiations pursued between the Government of the French Republic and the Government of His Majesty in Great Britain having given proof of their accord on a common attitude to be observed in regard to the situation in Spain, I have the honor in conformity with the proposal laid before the other European Governments, and mindful of the initiatives already taken unilaterally by the Government of France, to make to your Excellency the following declaration:

The Government of the French Republic,

Deploring the tragic events of which Spain is the threatre;

Resolved to abstain rigorously from all interference, direct or indirect, in the internal affairs of that country;

Animated by the desire to avoid every complication which might prejudice maintenance of good relations between nations,

Declares the following:

1. The French Government, in so far as it is concerned, prohibits direct or indirect exportation, re-exportation and transit, to a destination in Spain, the Spanish possessions or the Spanish zone of Morocco, of all arms, munitions and materials of war as well as all aircraft, assembled or dismantled, and all vessels of war;

2. This prohibition applies to contracts in process of execution;

3. The French Government will keep the other governments participating in this entente informed of all measures taken by it to give effect to the present declarations.

The French Government, in so far as it is concerned, will put this declaration into effect as soon as the Government of His Britannic Majesty, the German Government, the Italian Government, the Government of the U.S.S.R., and the Portuguese Government shall likewise have adhered to it.

As soon as the adhesions of the other governments concerned reach it, the French Government will take care to communicate them to the British Government as well as to the other interested Governments.

I have the honor, Mr. Ambassador, etc.

(Signed) Delbos

That same day, August 15, the British government, through its Ambassador in Paris, addressed a note to the French Foreign Minister that both in form and content was virtually identical with the original French declaration. This exchange of notes between Yvon Delbos and Sir George Clerk gave considerable impetus to the conclusion of a general agreement. Within a fortnight after the exchange, Germany, Italy, Soviet Russia, and Portugal, as well as most of the other interested powers, formally adhered to the nonintervention agreement.

On August 17 the German government, in a note to the French ambassador in Berlin, M. François-Poncet, indicated that it was prepared to adhere to the plan. However, the German note, omitting the pre-ambulatory reasons for making the declaration but repeating the three basic statements of policy of the French note, declared that the German government could not put this policy into effect until the Spanish government agreed to release the D-AMIM and "Governments of the other States which possess, in appreciable quantity, industries capable of producing the articles cited by the prohibition . . . likewise contract the same engagement and this engagement . . . be applied to delivery by individuals or by private societies." The note, moreover, inquired as to what measures would be taken by the interested powers to prevent the departure of volunteers for Spain. However, a week later, on August 24, the German government in another note to the French Ambassador in Berlin formally adhered to the nonintervention agreement, basing its adhesion on its note of August 17 but waiving the condition with respect to the D-AMIM.

Meanwhile, on August 21, the Italian government, in a note to the French ambassador in Rome, Count de Chambrun, had announced its adhesion to the nonintervention agreement. However, the Italian note, like the German note of August 17, did not contain the preambulatory reasons for the declaration. Moreover, the Italian note interpreted the phrase "indirect interference" of the original French declaration to mean the prohibition of subscription of funds and recruitment of volunteers for Spain. Yet, it declared that "the Italian Government, in accepting adherence to 'direct' non-intervention, has the honor, in consequence, to maintain its observations concerning 'indirect' non-intervention." The Italian note concluded with the statement that the Italian government deemed it essential that all important European states which produced arms join in the nonintervention plan.

The Portuguese government had also announced its formal adherence to the nonintervention agreement on August 21. However, the Portuguese note, somewhat anomalously in a declaration of neutrality and noninterference, stated that "the Portuguese Government deplores the events which are taking place in Spain and it formally censures the barbarous treatment of people by the communist and anarchist troops in areas which they control." The Portuguese government, moreover, made its adhesion to the agreement subject to a number of conditions and reservations. These included, beside the prohibition of subscription of funds and the recruitment of volunteers for Spain on the part of all the interested powers, the right of Portugal to act in its own defense "against all régimes of social subversion which might be established in Spain, if the necessity of safeguarding western civilization requires such a defense," and the right of Portugal to maintain "relations with central or local authorities which control, in fact, the government or administration in Spanish territory."

On August 23 the Soviet government formally adhered to the nonintervention agreement. The Soviet note was virtually identical with those of the French and British governments, repeating verbatim, *mutatis mutandis,* the preambulatory reasons for making the declaration and the three basic statements of policy of the original French declaration.

Having reached general agreement with respect to a policy of nonintervention in Spain, the next step to be taken by the interested powers was to establish some sort of central committee which could deal with the various problems which might arise under the plan. The suggestion to establish adequate supervision of the agreement first came from the Italian government. It was made by Foreign Minister Ciano in a conversation with the French ambassador in Rome, Count de Chambrun, as early as August 10, but Ciano's purpose in making it might well have been dilatory and, therefore, was not necessarily constructive. However, by the end of the month and with general agreement achieved, the French government, supported by the British government, earnestly sought the establishment of a supervisory committee. Berlin, however, was reluctant to accede to the idea, fearing that "the committee suggested by the French government might gradually develop into an agency of extended competence with control functions."

However, just as German Foreign Minister Constantin von Neurath had been able to prevail upon the Führer to permit the German government to announce its formal adherence to the nonintervention agreement on August 24 (the very day that the German government announced the extension of the period of military service from one to two years) and thus not to have it appear that Berlin was "sabotaging the whole matter," so the German Foreign Ministry, assured by the British chargé d'affaires in Berlin, Mr. Basil Newton, that "the work of the committee would not expand in an undesirable manner," was able to persuade Hitler to accede to the establishment of a supervisory committee in London. It appears that it was Dr. Hans Dieckhoff, at the time acting state secretary in the German Foreign Ministry, who supplied the initiative in this matter. In a letter dated August 29, 1936, to Baron von Neurath, Dieckhoff wrote that not only were the French and British governments in favor of the establishment of a supervisory committee but the Italian government was as well, provided that this committee were located in London and not in Paris. "Thus we would probably be quite alone in our negative attitude," said Dieckhoff. But he added:

I hardly believe that the plan could really entail any serious danger for us. The word "control" does not appear in the French note; according to François-Poncet's explanation, too, what was involved was primarily an exchange of information and a coordination. We ourselves, after all, can play a part in seeing that this London arrangement does not develop into a permanent political agency which might make trouble for us; and in this we can secure Italian and British support, too.

Naturally, we have to count on complaints of all kinds being brought up in London regarding failure to observe the obligation not to intervene, but we cannot avoid such complaints in any case. It can, in fact, only be agreeable to us if the center of gravity, which

after all has thus far been in Paris because of the French initiative, is transferred to London.

On September 9, 1936, the first meeting of the International Committee for the Application of the Agreement Regarding Non-Intervention in Spain was held at the British Foreign Office in London. Mr. W. S. Morrison of England was elected chairman of the committee, but he was soon succeeded by Lord Pymouth (Ivor Miles Windsor-Clive). Mr. Francis Hemming, also of England, was named secretary to the committee. At the second meeting of the committee, on September 14, a sub-committee to assist the chairman was created. It was composed of the representatives of Belgium, Czechoslovakia, France, Germany, Great Britain, Italy, Soviet Russia, Sweden, and, by September 28, Portugal. To this steering committee fell most of the real work of the London Non-Intervention Committee.

From the foregoing account of the conclusion of a general agreement and the establishment of a supervisory committee in London the inference is plain that the interested powers, particularly Germany, Italy, and Portugal, did not conceive of the nonintervention plan as a legal and moral instrument that would seriously limit the part they might seek to play in the Spanish drama nor of the London committee as other than an innocuous gathering of fainéant diplomats. In a report dated August 28, 1936, to the German Foreign Ministry, the German chargé d'affaires in Rome, Baron Johann von Plessen, wrote that Italian adherence to the nonintervention scheme came "sooner than was to be expected." The Baron believed that even the French Embassy was surprised by the Italian decision. The German added that he inferred from a remark made to him by the Italian under secretary of state, Giuseppe Bastianini, that the Italian government had come to believe that further delay in concluding the nonintervention agreement might benefit the Madrid government more than General Franco. Baron von Plessen then noted:

That the Italian government has attempted, by the way its reply has been formulated, to reserve far-reaching freedom of action for all contingencies is just as obvious as that it does not intend to abide by the declaration anyway.

The Italian note of adherence to the nonintervention agreement was, indeed, Machiavellian. It did not contain the preambulatory resolution of the original French note to refrain from all interference, direct or indirect, in Spanish internal affairs. The Italian note, moreover, interpreted the phrase "indirect interference" to mean such activities as the subscription of funds and the recruitment of volunteers for Spain. Thus, in adhering to "direct nonintervention" but maintaining its "observations" regarding "indirect nonintervention," the Italian government sought to limit the freedom of action with respect to both "direct" and "indirect" interference of those nations which in their notes of adherence embodied the aforementioned preambulatory resolution (ultimately, the majority of the twenty-seven participating states, including France, Great Britain, and Soviet Russia) while binding Italy only with respect to "direct intervention."

However, so little disturbed by this Italian maneuver was the French ambassador in Rome, Count de Chambrun, to whom the Italian note had been addressed, that he stated in a conversation with Mr. Kirk, the American chargé d'affaires in Rome, that he was "well satisfied" with the Italian note. Chambrun appeared particularly pleased that the Italian government maintained only "observations" and not "reservations" concerning "indirect nonintervention." British circles in Rome shared Chambrun's satisfaction.

As was indicated above, the German government in its note of adherence to the nonintervention agreement did not include the preambulatory reasons for making the declaration of the original French note, so that its position with respect to "indirect intervention" was not unlike that of Italy.

While the Portuguese note of August 21 declared that the Portuguese government would refrain from all interference, direct or indirect, in Spanish affairs, it contained enough important reservations not only to obviate the validity of this particular declaration but to render Portuguese participation itself virtually an empty gesture.

The attitude of the German government concerning the proper role and function of the London Non-Intervention Committee has already been discussed. On this matter, Rome was in substantial agreement with Berlin. Count Dino Grandi, the Italian ambassador in London and Italy's representative on the London Committee, received secret instructions "to do his best to give the committee's entire activity a purely platonic character." At the same time, Prince Otto Christian von Bismarck, the counselor of the German Embassy in London and Germany's representative on the London Committee, was instructed by Berlin to work closely with Count Grandi.

A close study of the documents pertaining to the nonintervention plan reveals that not only was sincere adherence to it not contemplated by at least some of the participating powers and that, objectively, it failed to prevent large-scale intervention in the Spanish conflict even after it had been strengthened by more stringent arrangements but that it intrinsically was not, and never really became, a legally binding obligation such as would have been the case if the nonintervention plan had been embodied in a formal treaty. It remained, therefore, little more than a moral commitment on the part of each of the participating powers. In discussing the status of the nonintervention agreement in international law, Norman J. Padelford noted:

It must be emphasized that the accord was not a formal international agreement or treaty in the sense that the participating states subscribed by signature and ratification to one written instrument. It was an "accord" only in a very loose form, a series of *unilateral declarations of intention* of the national policy which would be pursued. Departures from the accord cannot be condemned as violations of international law or of treaties. They constituted only deviations from a line of policy which each state suggested its readiness to follow for the time being. The fulfillment of the accord, or its enforcement in any particular state depended entirely upon the goodwill and coöperation of the authorities of that state, and upon the enaction and/or enforcement of such legislative, executive or administrative measures as were deemed to be desirable.

Certainly the continued and increasingly expanded intervention of Germany and Italy in the Spanish conflict constituted a violation of the spirit of the nonintervention agreement. Yet, those statesmen, publicists, and journalists in the Western democracies who raised a hue and cry about Italo-German violation of the nonintervention agreement were either victims of a terrible self-deception or parties to a huge hoax. For they successfully created the impression in the public mind that a hard and fast nonintervention agreement did exist and that while England and France faithfully adhered to it the fascist powers did not. Moreover, they successfully established the idea in the public mind that the task at hand was somehow to force the Germans and Italians to abide by the agreement. Thus, an emphasis was placed where it did not belong, for it was foolish, if not worse, to insist that an agreement that was little more than a moral commitment be regarded as a legally binding instrument. The real task at hand was either to establish an effective, legally binding instrument of nonintervention, and this forthwith, or to regain the freedom of action that had been unilaterally surrendered by the Western powers.

The conclusion is inescapable that the nonintervention scheme was cut from the same cloth as the partial economic sanctions imposed on Italy during the Italo-Ethiopian War, the inefficacy of the one matching the inadequacy of the other. It is not without significance that, with the warm approval of both Berlin and Rome, the Non-Intervention Committee came to sit in London and that its Chairman was as Englishman. With respect to the nonintervention agreement, it was the Quai d'Orsay which proposed but No. 10 Downing Street which disposed.

*   *   *

. . . The Condor Legion — the term applied to regular formations of German forces, including infantry, fighting on Spanish soil — came into existence on November 7, 1936. The rebel-held port of Cádiz was a beehive of activity in November, 1936, "owing to visits of numerous German vessels." Fully equipped contingents of artillery and infantry as well as aviation units, involving thousands of men, were disembarked. On November 17, some 1200 Germans, "some in khaki and boots," arrived in Sevilla, their equipment including "small touring cars of foreign design" and "field kitchens." Following the recognition of the Franco government on November 18, 1936, by the fascist powers, the flow of German men and equipment to rebel Spain was considerably accelerated. On December 1, 5000 Germans landed at Cádiz. At about the same time, 2500 Germans landed at Vigo. According to information received by the American ambassador to Spain, Claude G. Bowers, from American correspondents who had been with the rebel forces, Salamanca, where General Franco made his headquarters, resembled "a German military camp, German officers predominating." By the first week of January, 1937, the number of Germans fighting with the rebels was estimated at about 12,000, and approximately 80 per cent of the rebel air force was said to be German.

The Italians, like the Germans, continued unabatedly to assist the Spanish rebels both while the discussions which led to the nonintervention agreement were in progress and after a general agreement was concluded. On August 28, one week after Italy's formal adherence to the nonintervention agreement and on the very day

Rome placed a ban on the exportation of war materials to Spain, twelve Italian pilots and airplanes arrived at Vigo, proceeding at once to Burgos. On September 3, Madrid protested to the nonintervention powers against the arrival of additional Italian aircraft at Vigo.

A particularly flagrant violation of the Italian pledge not to interfere in Spanish internal affairs was the occupation of Majorca, the largest of the Balearic Islands, by Italian forces in early September, 1936. Majorca had been in the possession of rebel forces since the beginning of the insurrection, the military commander of the Balearic Islands with headquarters at Palma having been General Manuel Goded, the insurgent leader who was later captured and executed in Barcelona. The Catalans, upon suppressing the revolt in Catalonia, had dispatched an expedition to recover Majorca, but the effort had floundered against Italian air power. One of Francisco Largo Caballero's first acts upon becoming premier of the Spanish Republic on September 4, 1936, was to recall the Catalans fighting on the island. Majorca remained in the hands of the rebels throughout the war. However, with the arrival of thousands of Italian soldiers, sailors, and airmen, it became, in fact, an Italian military base. In a conversation with Herr Hans Frank, German minister without portfolio, at the Palazzo Venezia in Rome on September 23, 1936, Mussolini declared that much Italian blood had been shed in Spain and that "the Balearics were saved only by Italian men and Italian material."

Soviet Military Aid to the Republic

DAVID T. CATTELL

Professor Cattell, of the University of California at Los Angeles, made the first thorough study of the communist and Soviet roles in Spain. His work is particularly noteworthy for the inclusion of Russian language sources not previously studied by Western scholars. The following selection discusses principally the material and military aid supplied to the Republic by the Soviets.

The reader will want to ask himself what significant differences there may have been between international Communist aid and specifically Soviet aid. Also, combining the materials of the Survey and of Cattell, is it possible to judge the extent of Soviet influence on the conduct of the war and on the politics of Republican Spain?

B Y THE TIME the monarchy collapsed in 1931, the accusation of "Moscow agent" was already an old term in respect to the Left in Spain, as was the claim that Moscow was sending aid in the form of money and guns to Spanish revolutionaries. During the Asturian revolt of 1934 the cry reached a virtual din. The allegation was accepted by the Right as good propaganda and no one bothered to investigate the truth of the matter. Money was supposedly smuggled in on Russian ships, which were also reported to have landed arms on the Asturian coast. It is true that the Socialists, Anarchists, and Communists were all building up caches of arms and made little

From D. Cattell, *Communism and the Spanish Civil War* (Berkeley, 1955), pp. 69–79. Reprinted by permission of University of California Press.

attempt to deny it, though it is doubtful that they obtained them from the Soviet Union. Gerald Brenan, in his book *The Spanish Labyrinth,* says that the arms used in the October uprising originally came from the Spanish government's arsenals. "The principal supply had been ordered by Echevarrieta, the well-known Basque financier and a friend of Prieto, from the Consorcio de Fábricas Militares in 1932." The only known aid the Soviet Union did give to the Asturian workers was in funds raised in Russian factories to feed and clothe the survivors and the dependents of the revolt, but these funds did not reach Spain until after the revolt was over.

After the victory of the Popular Front in February, 1936, to no one's surprise the stories of Russian aid again began to circulate even before the July 19 uprising. After the beginning of the insurrection the propaganda machines of the Right issued reams of "evidence" of Soviet aid to the Republicans. It is difficult to check the so-called facts, but where it was possible to find the source it was usually a newspaper report or a rumor. Actually, there was little attempt by the Right to prove the existence of Soviet assistance. No attempt, for example, was made to send a group of unbiased investigators to check the rumors as was done by the Left. The reports seem to have been only propaganda to cover up the rebels' own outside source of supplies and to justify their use of foreign material when it was impossible to conceal it. It was, and still is, the favorite game of dictators to multiply the charges to such an extent that it is impossible to investigate them thoroughly and to blame the other side for what they are doing. In conclusion, it can be said that after carefully investigating the multitude of reports on Soviet material landed in Spain up to October, 1936, there are no grounds for believing the existence of this kind of aid. The very fact that there is plenty of proof of the presence of Russian aid after October, 1936, even though the Soviet Union was trying to conceal it, leads to the conclusion that if Russia had

given arms before this date more substantial evidence would be available.

Nationalist and Fascist reports on Soviet help after October, 1936, when there were good indications of Soviet war material from the Republican camp itself, were a peculiar combination of fact and fiction. Even where there seemed to have been some basis in fact, there were only meager attempts to cite evidence or indicate sources. An outstanding example of this is a speech by a master in the art of propaganda, Dr. Joseph Goebbels, in support of Franco. In the first part of the quotation below he uses figures which independent checking of other sources reveals were within reason (only altered in respect to time) and were probably based on good intelligence reports. Then, in the last sentence, he uses figures which appear completely out of line with the first figures he cited. The later figures were by his own evidence, therefore, exaggerated and made up for propaganda purposes.

. . . Within the short period of time from March 6 to May 14, 1937 — that is to say after the control plan had come into force — through the Dardanelles there passed 190 munition ships belonging to Soviet Russia and 88 ships flying the flag of the Red Party in Spain, on their way to Spanish harbours within the Red domination. These ships brought 162 tanks, 130 cannons, 86 aeroplanes, 395 motor transport cars, 12 anti-aircraft guns, 31,420 tons of other war material and munitions. During February and March 101 Russian Soviet aeroplanes were shipped from Reval to Spain. And on March 1st, 50 heavy guns from Soviet Russia were brought overland to Almansa. Recently one single large consignment of war material from Soviet Russia to the Reds in Spain included 100 heavy tanks, 500 medium-size tanks, 2,000 light tanks, 4,000 heavy machine guns, 6,000 light machine guns and 300 aeroplanes, with their pilots.

Soviet material assistance took two forms, relief and war material. Relief, consisting of food and clothing for women and children, started at the very beginning of the

Civil War. In every city and town in the Soviet Union meetings were held during the first weeks of the rebellion to demonstrate solidarity with the Spanish people. The pages of *Pravda* and *Izvestiia* were filled with speeches and pledges of help from the Russian people. On August 6, 1936, Secretary Shvernik of the All-Union Central Soviet of Trade Unions announced the sending of 12,145,000 rubles (over two million dollars) to the Spanish people collected from Russian workers. It was expected that in the month of August contributions would reach over four million dollars. The reasons for this immediate support for the Republican side are several. First, the Soviet Union had been watching all along the growth of the revolutionary situation in Spain, and as the alleged leader of world revolution she had to champion it for her own prestige. Since at first Russia was unwilling to commit herself in respect to armed aid, she had to make the most of the propaganda value of verbal solidarity and of supplies of food and clothing. On the other hand there appeared to be a genuine feeling of fellowship on the part of the Russian people with the Spanish masses which grew up spontaneously and was merely put to use by the Soviet government for its own purpose. Finally, Russia urged support of Spain because she wanted to arouse the democracies to aid the Spanish people. Russia feared a totalitarian regime in Spain which would tend to isolate France, the new keystone of Russia's security system. As a result the Soviet government itself actively encouraged and sponsored the collection of funds for Spain.

With the adherence of the Soviet Union to the Non-Intervention Pact at the end of August, the collection of relief funds for Spain was allowed to lag, in order not to give grounds to the claim of the Fascist powers that the Soviet Union was violating the pact. Some authorities have alleged it was due to French pressure that the collections stopped. When it became obvious, however, by the middle of September,

1936, that Germany and Italy had not stopped supplying the rebels, the Soviet government launched a new campaign for funds for Spain. The newspapers again were filled with reports of meetings, letters, and contributions. By October, the collection had reached a total of 47,600,000 rubles. And by the end of October, five ships laden with food had been sent to Spain from the port of Odessa.

Not only were the Communists active in collecting in the Soviet Union but through Communist-sponsored organizations throughout the world large sums were collected for Spain. Besides the already established societies the Communists created a new network of organizations solely for the support of Spain, so that those people who would not work through a Communist organization could still aid Spain. A typical organization was the *Comité International d' Aide au Peuple Espagnol* in Paris, which between August, 1936, and June, 1938, had collected over half a million dollars. It would be difficult to estimate how much money was given through the Communist parties and organizations, as there is no complete accounting and much of it was sent in the form of food. It would not, however, be an exaggeration to say that the total aid was in the neighborhood of fifty million dollars.

This source of food and clothing was extremely important to the welfare of the Spanish Republic. The most important wheat and dairy area had fallen to the rebels and the Republican regions were generally deficient in food, having a surplus of oranges and wine only. Furthermore, the collectivization program and alteration of the usual channels of trade in the early months of the war had greatly reduced agricultural production and exchange. Consequently, Spain found herself approaching the winter of 1936 with a shortage of food, even after the channels of trade and transport had been restored. This made outside contributions very helpful, especially since Spain did not have the opportunity to earn foreign exchange because most of her production was being used for war. The importance of this non-military aid from the Soviet Union can be seen in the USSR's trade with Spain as published by the Soviet government: In the course of the first six months of 1937, Russia exported to Spain 322,000 tons (51,442,000 rubles) compared with 47,000 tons (2,582,000 rubles) for the same period in 1936, thus making Spain Russia's second best customer (Great Britain being first with over 100,000,000 rubles). Imports from Spain went from 900,000 rubles to 16,934,000 rubles. From January to October, 1937, the Russians exported to Spain 105,283 tons of coal, 163,841 tons of oil products, 85,739 tons of grain, 7,864 tons of trucks, 30,802 tons of fertilizer, and 16,687 tons of cotton. Soviet imports from Spain were only 17,303 tons of lead and 26,621 tons of oranges and lemons.

Although the Soviet Union well publicized the fact that relief aid was being given by her people to Spain, the sending of military aid was never acknowledged. The Soviet government came as close as it ever did in admitting it was proposing to send military help when the Russian representative to the Non-Intervention Committee sent a note to the secretary of the committee saying, "The Soviet Government is therefore compelled to declare that if violations of the Agreement for Non-Intervention are not immediately stopped the Soviet Government will consider itself free from the obligations arising out of that agreement." Beyond this, no official Communist publication ever mentioned the sending of military equipment. Frequently, however, the Communist Party of Spain mentioned Soviet succor but did not designate exactly to what they were referring. By the importance they ascribed to it in the saving of Spain, military aid must have been included. For example, José Díaz' speech on November 13, 1937:

The decisive importance of the aid from the Soviet Union is recognized by all our people.

As expressed very well by Señor Martínez Barrio, President of the Cortes and of the Union Republican Party, without the aid of the Soviet Union our Republic would not still exist today. This is certain. The aid came at just that moment which permitted us to overcome the critical hour of our struggle and resolve the great problems of the war with vigor. Only the Soviet Union understood, at that tragic moment that the cause of peace of the entire world was at stake. . . .

At first the Soviet Union tried to keep the sending of military supplies a complete secret, but the numerous reporters throughout Loyalist Spain had few restrictions placed upon them which, combined with the inability of the Spanish government employees to maintain the secret, made all efforts at concealment futile. As a result, the Soviet Union continued to maintain official ignorance, but in unofficial declarations made full use of the propaganda value of being the only great power to help democratic Spain. Communist apologists followed this line and published quite freely the fact that the Soviet Union was sending military aid.

The first time Soviet equipment was used in the fight against the Nationalists was about November 7, 1936, in the siege of Madrid when the enemy was already in the suburbs. José Martín Blázquez reports that the first Russian supplies arrived at the beginning of October, at Alicante. This fits in very closely with November 7 as the first day of the appearance of Russian equipment in the form of planes seen in the fighting. Walter Krivitsky, in his book *In Stalin's Secret Service,* mentioned that the Politbureau of the Communist party of the USSR made the decision to intervene with arms in the Spanish conflict at the end of August or the first part of September, which is also in keeping with the arrival of material during the first part of October and its use at the beginning of November. Krivitsky stated that the sending of material was divided into three sections. The first part was headed by the Soviet army which sent technicians and pilots to supervise the use of the matériel. In the absence of skilled Spanish personnel, Soviet drivers were used in the tanks and Soviet pilots in the planes. Otherwise, no Soviet personnel were to enter combat but were merely to serve as technical advisers. Krivitsky reports that Stalin had warned all his men: "Stay out of range of the artillery fire!" This order follows the reports of other observers in Spain. Stalin had no desire to expend the skill of his army in Spain when at home there was a great shortage of technicians and trained soldiers. He also did not want to give any grounds to the accusations that a Soviet army was invading Spain since Italian troops were being accused of this by the Republicans. Stalin, under no circumstances, wanted to be charged with being an aggressor. He kept within the provision of international law which allowed for the supplying of arms to the legitimate government in a civil war, though in doing so he violated the Non-Intervention Pact. It is also probable that he feared defeat of Russian soldiers would lower his prestige and might even force Russia into war with Germany. Furthermore, to put his troops into action in Spain would only have begun an undeclared war between Russian, German, and Italian troops.

The second section of Russian succor for Spain was under the *GPU* (secret police) in Russia and headed by Captain Oulansky. This provided for the clandestine supplying of material from Russia through the port of Odessa to Spain. The main problem was to prevent knowledge of the traffic going to foreign capitals and in this respect the Russians were only partially successful. The German Consulate at Odessa reported the loading of ships bound presumably for Spain during October and November, 1936. At first it was planned to use only Spanish ships, but because of the small number available, Soviet ships had to be used.

The third branch of Communist arms trade with Spain was through a system of Communist International agents and companies under Krivitsky himself. It was their purpose to act as agents for the Spanish government, using their connections and world organization to buy war materials from wherever possible in the world. Krivitsky stated, "We made large purchases from the Skoda works in Czechoslovakia, from several firms in France, from others in Poland and Holland. Such is the nature of the munitions trade that we even bought arms in Nazi Germany. I sent an agent representing a Dutch firm of ours to Hamburg, where we had ascertained that quantities of somewhat obsolete rifles and machine guns were for sale. The director of the German firm was interested in nothing but the price, the bank references and legal papers of consignment."

To answer the question of how much material Russia sent to the Loyalists is by no means easy. With the delivery of the arms to Spain, Russian control did not end, and the tendency was to move all the material into fields and camps set aside for the Russians. These depots were under exclusive Russian or Communist control and even high Spanish government officials did not appear to know what they contained. In these depots supplies remained, to be doled out and used as the Russian advisers thought fit. Colonel Casado, in his book *The Last Days of Madrid*, relates:

. . . I can state clearly that during the whole war neither the Air Force nor the Tank Corps was controlled by the Minister of National Defense, nor in consequence by the Central General Staff. The Minister and his Staff were not even aware of the quantity and types of their machines and only knew the situation of those which were used in actual operations. In the same way the Minister and his Staff were not aware of the situation, and even of the existence, of a great number of unknown "flying fields" (aerodromes) maintained in secret by the "friendly [Russian] advisers" and certain of the Aviation Chiefs who were entirely in their confidence.

José Martín Blázquez, on the other hand, gives the impression, "In the Air Force we exercise full control. The Russians are very tactful, and realize that we wouldn't take orders from them." The evidence available does not support Martín Blázquez, however. A study of the statements made by the top leaders in the Loyalist government and discussion with several of them reveals the fact that, although all were aware of Soviet arms, none knew how much was sent or where the material was. Indalecio Prieto, Minister of Marine and Air or Minister of Defense for most of the war, declared, "In regard to keeping accounts on Russian aid, never was it carried out with intransigence because on numerous occasions it was permitted the Sub-Secretaries of Armament and Aviation [usually Communists] sign invoices on matériel which had not even arrived and furthermore I, myself, have signed invoices under such conditions." Consequently, it is almost impossible to make an intelligent estimate of the quantity of material. The only way to arrive at any evaluation is to rely on reports of observers in Spain, on Nationalist reports; and on intelligence reports of the Fascist powers.

From the reporting of foreign observers one gets the impression that aid from the Soviet Union never reached the magnitude of Italian and German supplies to Franco. Nor was Spain ever used extensively by Russia as a training ground for troops, or as a laboratory to test new equipment and techniques, as she was by Italy and Germany. This empirical judgment agrees with the conclusion arrived at by inductive reasoning. In contrast to Germany and especially Italy, the Russian supply lines to Spain were long and circuitous. Furthermore, shipments from Russia to Spain were easily observable in the various narrows through which the ships had to pass. Nationalist and Italian submarines and planes plotted the course of Russian ships through the Mediterranean, and at Loyalist ports rebel observers watched the unloading of the ships. As a result it was difficult for Russia to hide her shipments.

To Germany and Italy the Non-Intervention Pact was merely a scrap of paper. They tried to stall their fulfillment of the agreement as long as possible and at the same time keep the democratic powers from going to the aid of the Loyalists. This they could easily do by merely throwing out a few false promises in the Non-Intervention Committee. To Russia, on the other hand, it was important and essential that in breaking the agreement she should not in any way alienate her potential partners, the Western democracies, and that the West should not lose faith in Russia as an ally because she failed to abide by the pact. Consequently, it was particularly important to Russia that she hide her activities in Spain.

Russia was perhaps also fearful of consigning too much to Spain if perchance a world war suddenly broke out, in which case all her commitments to Spain would have been immediately isolated and lost. In the event of a world war, the long lines of communication between Russia and Spain would have been impossible to maintain in terms of the military advantage obtained. Italy, however, would have been in an excellent position to continue her aid and thus menace France on her Spanish frontier and disrupt her African communications.

In the grand strategy of Italy and Germany for the conquest of Europe, Spain played an important role as a training ground, as a base, and as a pincer against France. The outcome of the Spanish conflict, therefore, was of particular importance to them. The Soviet Union entered the Spanish war as a side issue in her security system. In a war with the Fascist powers, Spain could serve no immediate role in the defense of Russia. In addition, Soviet supplies were kept to a minimum by the activities of the Nationalist and Italian submarines which carried on an extensive war against all Republican trade. Consequently, it is not surprising that the observations by correspondents should conclude that Russia's aid to the Republicans never reached the proportions of Fascist aid to Franco.

From Italian and German intelligence reports, from information reported by the Secretary of the Sea Observation Plan of the Non-Intervention Committee, and from newspaper reports some estimate can be made of the amount of shipping from Russia to Spain. From the middle of October, 1936, to the inauguration of the Non-Intervention Control Scheme on April 20, 1937, there left Russia for Spain between thirty and forty ships per month of varying tonnages. Over half the ships were Russian-owned and the rest were Spanish, plus a few Greek and Scandinavian. None of the ships carried war material exclusively, because legitimate cargo was needed to disguise the arms and because Spain had good use for legitimate cargo as well as for war material. Half or more of each shipload was food, clothing, medicines, fuel oil, or transport trucks; all legal cargo under the Non-Intervention Pact. The rest consisted of arms, ammunition, tanks, and planes.

By the time the Non-Intervention Control Scheme went into effect in April, 1937, there was a considerable drop in the shipments to Spain. Piracy had begun in the Mediterranean at the end of 1936 and became more and more serious during 1937. At the time it was difficult to place the blame because the sinkings were made by submarine or by unmarked airplanes, but it is now known that the attacks were carried out primarily by the Nationalists and Italians to cut down shipments to Republican Spain and to stop Russia from sending aid. The piracy had the desired effect. The foreign trade of Loyalist Spain was reduced considerably, and Russia became more and more fearful of losing her none too plentiful merchant marine and of "becoming too deeply involved in a crisis over the sinkings of Soviet ships. After the sinking of the *Komsomol* in December, 1936, Russian ships were used less and less to supply Spain. By the time of the inauguration of the control scheme,

use of Soviet ships for Spanish ports had stopped completely. Russia did not want to participate in the control scheme in any way. Consequently, no Russian ships were ever reported by the intelligence system of the Non-Intervention Committee as going legally or illegally to Spain. Since the Spanish government's shipping facilities were limited, and since only a few foreign companies were willing to ship illegally at very high costs, the elimination of Soviet ships brought a considerable decrease in the supplies going to Spain. Another factor to be considered is that in 1936 and the early part of 1937, when Spain was in a state of turmoil, when the Nationalists were winning all the victories and Madrid was seriously threatened, there was an immediate need of large quantities of arms to save the Loyalists. With the stabilizing of the fronts, the development of armament industries, and the general improvement of conditions in Republican Spain during 1937, the Loyalists were in a position to supply their own forces with at least part of their equipment, and the urgency of Soviet aid consequently decreased.

From Nationalist sources some idea can be gathered as to the proportion of Russian material in relation to that from other sources. The Nationalists claimed that between August, 1936 and April, 1937, 759 planes were delivered intact to the Loyalists. Of these 46 per cent came from the Soviet Union, 28 per cent from France, and the remaining 26 per cent from various other countries. Reports reaching the Department of State in Washington in March of 1937, on the other hand, indicated that Russian planes accounted for 92 per cent of the Loyalist Air Force. These two sources are not necessarily incompatible, however, because one set of figures is for the strength of the air force in March, and the other set is for deliveries up to August, 1937. The differences can also be explained by the fact that after February, 1937, the Soviet Union decreased her own shipments to the Loyalists, making it necessary for them to find aircraft elsewhere. For this, however, they had the help of Communist agents throughout the world, as discussed above. In any case it is clear that by far the largest supplier of aircraft to the Republicans was Russia.

By August, 1937, the Nationalists listed the following equipment as part of the foreign arms still usable which had been captured in the campaigns:

318	French machine guns
565	Foreign machine guns of varying types
948	Russian machine guns
954	Spare gun barrels (various)
1,358	French machine rifles
2,600,000	Cartridges for 8-mm Lebels (French)
120,000	Loaders for French machine rifles
2,800	French rifles
12,575	Russian rifles (two types)
886	Czech rifles
3,852	Mexican rifles
4,875,000	Cartridges for Russian rifles
24	French mortars (stock type)
53	37-mm French guns
32	75-mm French guns
16	155-mm French guns
18	124-mm Russian guns
52,000	Shells (French and Russian)
110	Russian tanks

Thus, using Hericourt's figures above as a basis, it can be estimated that of the foreign arms furnished, the Russians supplied about 100 per cent of the tanks, 50 per cent of the machine guns, 60 per cent of the rifles, and only about 15 per cent of the larger guns. France supplied about 20 per cent of the machine guns, 20 per cent of the rifles, and 85 per cent of the larger guns.

In analyzing the figures above, certain factors must be kept in mind. First, the figures do not include the Spanish-made material which admittedly at this time was not too great. A large quantity of the French-made material can be explained by prewar supply commitments, as before the war France had an agreement with Spain to supply her with the major portion of her war material. Furthermore the material sent by the Communists does not include only that made in the Soviet Union but also other material sent through Comintern agents. In addition, the Spanish, under Soviet direction, had begun manufacturing Soviet-type material. As a result Russian *Chato* airplanes and rifles were coming off the assembly lines in Spain, though by August of 1937 it is doubtful if large quantities had yet been produced in Spain. Finally, it is impossible to check the Nationalist figures for accuracy though they seem to agree with other evidence available.

From the figures above, the broad conclusion can be drawn that during the first days of the war about half the equipment and all the tanks used by the Spanish Loyalists came from Communist sources. This material in the beginning saved Republican Spain, since without it there is little doubt that Franco, with German and Italian help, would have been successful, perhaps as early as the end of 1936.

Authorities disagree as to when the Soviet Union ceased to send material to Spain. Again there is no absolute evidence because of the shroud of secrecy which accompanied all Soviet assistance. Some have put the end as early as the beginning of 1937. It is certainly true that less and less is heard of Soviet aid after this time. But from events in Spain and the growing power of the Communists, it would seem that supplies did not end abruptly. The maximum Loyalist military strength was reached only in December, 1937, when they launched their major offensive against the rebels in the direction of Teruel. The scarce but continued evidence from the Axis' intelligence reports and newspaper accounts leads to the conclusion that Russian aid continued after the beginning of 1937. Moreover, in the numerous accounts by government leaders and other participants on the Loyalist side in the war there is no mention of Soviet aid ending at this time. Certainly if the substantial flow of Soviet aid had come to a halt, its absence would have been noticed by at least some of the participants. Likewise, by 1937 the Soviet Union still appeared not to have lost hope of the democracies coming to the aid of the Loyalists. It was only after the continued procrastination of the West in the Non-Intervention Committee during 1937, that Russia was convinced the Western democracies would not be aroused by their own interest in Spain to protect the Republican government. It would seem that aid probably did not cease until the middle of 1938. The German Foreign Of-fice documents mention Russian aid during April, 1938, and the promise of continued support. By the summer of 1938, however, the military situation was such that the victory of Franco seemed assured. His offensive along the Ebro in the spring had been successful in cutting the Loyalist territory in two and showed that the Republican troops, in spite of strides toward a modern and efficient army, were not a match for the Nationalist army. Further, the Munich crisis was turning Russia's attention elsewhere. One indirect indication of the end of Russian aid was the withdrawal of the International Brigade from Spain in the summer and autumn of 1938.

Fact and Propaganda Concerning
the Barcelona Uprising

GEORGE ORWELL

In May, 1937, long accumulating tensions within the Popular Front led to several days of sporadic street fighting in Barcelona. Left Socialists, anarchists, and anti-Stalinist communists fought against Right Socialists, Communists, and "fellow travelers." The late George Orwell, who in England belonged to the Independent Labour Party, had volunteered to serve with the P.O.U.M. militia in Aragon, and by coincidence he became involved in the Barcelona street fighting. After his return to England he studied carefully the newspaper accounts of the days through which he had lived personally. The following selection summarizes the events and then proceeds to a masterly analysis of the ideological confusions and propaganda battles which prevented objective reporting of the struggle in the Spanish and world press. For explanation of the various party initials, see the list of definitions above, page xii.

Orwell's account raises a number of fascinating questions. On what grounds did the Communists try to blame the Barcelona fighting on the P.O.U.M. and the Trotskyists? What was the importance, in the international context, of emphasizing the adjective "Trotskyist"? What were the weaknesses of the Communist case from a factual point of view? How might both the events and their propaganda treatment have affected attitudes towards the Civil War in the democratic countries?

I T WILL NEVER BE POSSIBLE to get a completely accurate and unbiased account of the Barcelona fighting, because the necessary records do not exist. Future historians will have nothing to go upon except a mass of accusations and party propaganda. I myself have little data beyond what I saw with my own eyes and what I have learned from other eye-witnesses whom I believe to be reliable. I can, however, contradict some of the more flagrant lies and help to get the affair into some kind of perspective.

First of all, what actually happened?

For some time past there had been tension throughout Catalonia. In earlier chapters of this book I have given some account of the struggle between Communists and Anarchists. By May, 1937 things had reached a point at which some kind of violent outbreak could be regarded as inevitable. The immediate cause of friction was the Government's order to surrender all private weapons, coinciding with the decision to build up a heavily-armed "non-political" police-force from which trade union members were to be excluded. The meaning of this was obvious to everyone; and it was also obvious that the next move would be the taking over of some of the key industries controlled by the C.N.T. In addition there was a certain amount of resentment among the working classes because of the growing contrast of wealth and poverty and a general vague feeling that the revolution had been sabotaged. Many people were agreeably surprised when there was no rioting on 1 May. On 3

May the Government decided to take over the Telephone Exchange, which had been operated since the beginning of the war mainly by C.N.T. workers; it was alleged that it was badly run and that official calls were being tapped. Salas, the Chief of Police (who may or may not have been exceeding his orders), sent three lorry-loads of armed Civil Guards to seize the building, while the streets outside were cleared by armed police in civilian clothes. At about the same time bands of Civil Guards seized various other buildings in strategic spots. Whatever the real intention may have been, there was a widespread belief that this was the signal for a general attack on the C.N.T. by the Civil Guards and the P.S.U.C. (Communists and Socialists). The word flew round the town that the workers' buildings were being attacked, armed Anarchists appeared on the streets, work ceased, and fighting broke out immediately. That night and the next morning barricades were built all over the town, and there was no break in the fighting until the morning of 6 May. The fighting was, however, mainly defensive on both sides. Buildings were besieged, but, so far as I know, none were stormed, and there was no use of artillery. Roughly speaking, the C.N.T.-F.A.I.-P.O.U.M. forces held the working-class suburbs, and the armed police-forces and the P.S.U.C. held the central and official portion of the town. On 6 May there was an armistice, but fighting soon broke out again, probably because of premature attempts by Civil Guards to disarm C.N.T. workers. Next morning, however, the people began to leave the barricades of their own accord. Up till, roughly, the night of 5 May the C.N.T. had had the better of it, and large numbers of Civil Guards had surrendered. But there was no generally accepted leadership and no fixed plan—indeed, so far as one could judge, no plan at all except a vague determination to resist the Civil Guards. The official leaders of the C.N.T. had joined with those of the U.G.T. in imploring everyone to

go back to work; above all, food was running short. In such circumstances nobody was sure enough of the issue to go on fighting. By the afternoon of 7 May conditions were almost normal. That evening six thousand Assault Guards, sent by sea from Valencia, arrived and took control of the town. The Government issued an order for the surrender of all arms except those held by the regular forces, and during the next few days large numbers of arms were seized. The casualties during the fighting were officially given out as four hundred killed and about a thousand wounded. Four hundred killed is possibly an exaggeration, but as there is no way of verifying this we must accept it as accurate. . . .

In the Communist and pro-Communist press the entire blame for the Barcelona fighting was laid upon the P.O.U.M. The affair was represented not as a spontaneous outbreak, but as a deliberate, planned insurrection against the Government, engineered solely by the P.O.U.M. with the aid of a few misguided "uncontrollables." More than this, it was definitely a Fascist plot, carried out under Fascist orders with the idea of starting civil war in the rear and thus paralyzing the Government. The P.O.U.M. was "Franco's Fifth Column" —a "Trotskyist" organization working in league with the Fascists. According to the *Daily Worker* (11 May):

The German and Italian agents, who poured into Barcelona ostensibly to "prepare" the notorious "Congress of the Fourth International," had one big task. It was this:

They were — in co-operation with the local Trotskyists — to prepare a situation of disorder and bloodshed, in which it would be possible for the Germans and Italians to declare that they were "unable to exercise naval control of the Catalan coasts effectively because of the disorder prevailing in Barcelona" and were, therefore, "unable to do otherwise than land forces in Barcelona."

In other words, what was being prepared was a situation in which the German and Italian Governments could land troops or marines quite openly on the Catalan coasts, declaring that they were doing so "in order to preserve order." . . .

The instrument for all this lay ready to hand for the Germans and Italians in the shape of the Trotskyist organization known as the P.O.U.M.

The P.O.U.M., acting in co-operation with well-known criminal elements, and with certain other deluded persons in the Anarchist organizations planned, organized and led the attack in the rearguard, accurately timed to coincide with the attack on the front at Bilbao, etc., etc.

Later in the article the Barcelona fighting becomes "the P.O.U.M. attack," and in another article in the same issue it is stated that there is "no doubt that it is at the door of the P.O.U.M. that the responsibility for the bloodshed in Catalonia must be laid." *Inprecor*[1] (29 May) states that those who erected the barricades in Barcelona were "only members of the P.O.U.M organized from that party for this purpose."

I could quote a great deal more, but this is clear enough. The P.O.U.M. was wholly responsible and the P.O.U.M. was acting under Fascist orders. In a moment I will give some more extracts from the accounts that appeared in the Communist press; it will be seen that they are so self-contradictory as to be completely worthless. But before doing so it is worth pointing to several *a priori* reasons why this version of the May fighting as a Fascist rising engineered by the P.O.U.M. is next door to incredible.

(i) The P.O.U.M. had not the numbers or influence to provoke disorders of this magnitude. Still less had it the power to call a general strike. It was a political organization with no very definite footing in the trade unions, and it would have been hardly more capable of producing a strike throughout Barcelona than (say) the

English Communist Party would be of producing a general strike throughout Glasgow. As I said earlier, the attitude of the P.O.U.M. leaders may have helped to prolong the fighting to some extent; but they could not have originated it even if they had wanted to.

(ii) The alleged Fascist plot rests on bare assertion and all the evidence points in the other direction. We are told that the plan was for the German and Italian governments to land troops in Catalonia; but no German or Italian troopships approached the coast. As to the "Congress of the Fourth International" and the "German and Italian agents," they are pure myth. So far as I know there had not even been any talk of a Congress of the Fourth International. There were vague plans for a Congress of the P.O.U.M. and its brother-parties (English I.L.P., German S.A.P., etc., etc.); this had been tentatively fixed for some time in July — two months later — and not a single delegate had yet arrived. The "German and Italian agents" have no existence outside the pages of the *Daily Worker*. Anyone who crossed the frontier at that time knows that it was not so easy to "pour" into Spain, or out of it, for that matter.

(iii) Nothing happened either at Lerida, the chief stronghold of the P.O.U.M., or at the front. It is obvious that if the P.O.U.M. leaders had wanted to aid the Fascists they would have ordered their militia to walk out of the line and let the Fascists through. But nothing of the kind was done or suggested. Nor were any extra men brought out of the line beforehand, though it would have been easy enough to smuggle, say, a thousand or two thousand men back to Barcelona on various pretexts. And there was no attempt even at indirect sabotage of the front. The transport of food, munitions, and so forth continued as usual; I verified this by inquiry afterwards. Above all, a planned rising of the kind suggested would have needed months of preparation, subversive propaganda among the militia, and so forth. But

[1] International Press Correspondence, an unofficial but clearly Communist-run news service. [Editor's note.]

there was no sign or rumour of any such thing. The fact that the militia at the front played no part in the "rising" should be conclusive. If the P.O.U.M. were really planning a *coup d'état* it is inconceivable that they would not have used the ten thousand or so armed men who were the only striking force they had.

It will be clear enough from this that the Communist thesis of a P.O.U.M. "rising" under Fascist orders rests on less than no evidence. I will add a few more extracts from the Communist press. The Communist accounts of the opening incident, the raid on the Telephone Exchange, are illuminating; they agree in nothing except in putting the blame on the other side. It is noticeable that in the English Communist papers the blame is put first upon the Anarchists and only later upon the P.O.U.M. There is a fairly obvious reason for this. Not everyone in England has heard of "Trotskyism," whereas every English-speaking person shudders at the name of "Anarchist." Let it once be known that "Anarchists" are implicated, and the right atmosphere of prejudice is established; after that the blame can safely be transferred to the "Trotskyists." The *Daily Worker* begins thus (6 May):

A minority gang of Anarchists on Monday and Tuesday seized and attempted to hold the telephone and telegram buildings, and started firing into the street.

There is nothing like starting off with a reversal of roles. The Civil Guards attack a building held by the C.N.T.; so the C.N.T. are represented as attacking their own building — attacking themselves, in fact. On the other hand, the *Daily Worker* of 11 May states:

The Left Catalan Minister of Public Security, Aiguade, and the United Socialist General Commissar of Public Order, Rodríguez Sallas, sent the armed republican police into the Telefonica building to disarm the employees there, most of them members of C.N.T. unions.

This does not seem to agree very well with the first statement; nevertheless the *Daily Worker* contains no admission that the first statement was wrong. The *Daily Worker* of 11 May states that the leaflets of the Friends of Durruti, which were disowned by the C.N.T., appeared on 4 May and 5 May, during the fighting. *Inprecor* (22 May) states that they appeared on 3 May, *before* the fighting, and adds that "in view of these facts" (the appearance of various leaflets):

The police, led by the Prefect of Police in person, occupied the central telephone exchange in the afternoon of May 3rd. The police were shot at while discharging their duty. This was the signal for the provocateurs to begin shooting affrays all over the city.

And here is *Inprecor* for 29 May:

At three o'clock in the afternoon the Commissar for Public Security, Comrade Sallas, went to the Telephone Exchange, which on the previous night had been occupied by 50 members of the P.O.U.M. and various uncontrollable elements.

This seems rather curious. The occupation of the Telephone Exchange by 50 P.O.U.M. members is what one might call a picturesque circumstance, and one would have expected somebody to notice it at the time. Yet it appears that it was only discovered three or four weeks later. In another issue of *Inprecor* the 50 P.O.U.M. members become 50 P.O.U.M. militiamen. It would be difficult to pack together more contradictions than are contained in these few short passages. At one moment the C.N.T. are attacking the Telephone Exchange, the next they are being attacked there; a leaflet appears before the seizure of the Telephone Exchange and is the cause of it, or, alternatively, appears afterwards and is the result of it; the people in the Telephone Exchange are alternatively C.N.T. members and P.O.U.M. members — and so on. And in a still later issue of the *Daily Worker* (3 June) Mr. J. R. Campbell informs us that the Government only seized the Telephone Exchange because the barricades were already erected!

For reasons of space I have taken only the reports of one incident, but the same discrepancies run all through the accounts in the Communist press. In addition there are various statements which are obviously pure fabrication. Here for instance is something quoted by the *Daily Worker* (7 May) and said to have been issued by the Spanish Embassy in Paris:

A significant feature of the uprising has been that the old monarchist flag was flown from the balcony of various houses in Barcelona, doubtless in the belief that those who took part in the rising had become masters of the situation.

The *Daily Worker* very probably reprinted this statement in good faith, but those responsible for it at the Spanish Embassy must have been quite deliberately lying. Any Spaniard would understand the internal situation better than that. A monarchist flag in Barcelona! It was the one thing that could have united the warring factions in a moment. Even the Communists on the spot were obliged to smile when they read about it. It is the same with the reports in the various Communist papers upon the arms supposed to have been used by the P.O.U.M. during the "rising." They would be credible only if one knew nothing whatever of the facts. In the *Daily Worker* of 17 May Mr. Frank Pitcairn states:

There were actually all sorts of arms used by them in the outrage. There were the arms which they have been stealing for months past, and hidden, and there were arms such as tanks, which they stole from the barracks just at the beginning of the rising. It is clear that scores of machine guns and several thousand rifles are still in their possession.

Inprecor (29 May) also states:

On May 3rd the P.O.U.M. had at its disposal some dozens of machine guns and several thousand rifles. . . . On the Plaza d'Espagna the Trotskyists brought into action batteries of "75" guns which were destined for the front in Aragon and which the militia had carefully concealed on their premises.

Mr. Pitcairn does not tell us how and when it became clear that the P.O.U.M. possessed scores of machine-guns and several thousand rifles. I have given an estimate of the guns which were at three of the principal P.O.U.M. buildings — about eighty rifles, a few bombs, and no machine-guns; i.e. about sufficient for the armed guards which, at that time, all the political parties placed on their buildings. It seems strange that afterwards, when the P.O.U.M. was suppressed and all its buildings seized, these thousands of weapons never came to light; especially the tanks and field-guns, which are not the kind of thing that can be hidden up the chimney. But what is revealing in the two statements above is the complete ignorance they display of the local circumstances. According to Mr. Pitcairn the P.O.U.M. stole tanks "from the barracks." He does not tell us which barracks. The P.O.U.M. militiamen who were in Barcelona (now comparatively few, as direct recruitment to the party militias had ceased) shared the Lenin Barracks with a considerably larger number of Popular Army troops. Mr. Pitcairn is asking us to believe, therefore, that the P.O.U.M. stole tanks with the connivance of the Popular Army. It is the same with the "premises" on which the 75-mm. guns were concealed. There is no mention of where these "premises" were. Those batteries of guns, firing on the Plaza de España, appeared in many newspaper reports, but I think we can say with certainty that they never existed. As I mentioned earlier, I heard no artillery-fire during the fighting, though the Plaza de España was only a mile or so away. A few days later I examined the Plaza de España and could find no buildings that showed marks of shell-fire. And an eye-witness who was in that neighbourhood throughout the fighting declares that no guns ever appeared there. (Incidentally, the tale of the stolen guns may have originated with Antonov-Ovseenko, the Russian Consul-General. He, at any rate, communicated it to a well-known English journalist, who afterwards repeated it in good faith in a weekly paper. Antonov-Ovseenko has since been "purged." How this would affect his credibility I do not know.) The truth is, of course, that these tales about tanks, field-guns, and so forth have only been invented because otherwise it is difficult to reconcile the scale of the Barcelona fighting with the P.O.U.M.'s small numbers. It was necessary to claim that the P.O.U.M. was wholly responsible for the fighting; it was also necessary to claim that it was an insignificant party with no following and "numbered only a few thousand members," according to *Inprecor*. The only hope of making both statements credible was to pretend that the P.O.U.M. had all the weapons of a modern mechanized army. . . .

It is true that some of the attacks in the Communist Press said, rather grudgingly, that only the P.O.U.M. leaders were in Fascist pay, and not the rank and file. But this was merely an attempt to detach the rank and file from their leaders. The nature of the accusations implied that ordinary members, militiamen, and so forth, were all in the plot together; for it was obvious that if Nin, Gorkín, and the others were really in Fascist pay, it was more likely to be known to their followers, who were in contact with them, than to journalists in London, Paris, and New York. And in any case, when the P.O.U.M. was suppressed the Communist-controlled secret police acted on the assumption that all were guilty alike and arrested everyone connected with the P.O.U.M. whom they could lay hands on, including even wounded men, hospital nurses, wives of P.O.U.M. members and in some cases, even children.

Finally, on 15–16 June, the P.O.U.M.

was suppressed and declared an illegal organization. This was one of the first acts of the Negrín Government which came into office in May. When the Executive Committee of the P.O.U.M. had been thrown into jail, the Communist Press produced what purported to be the discovery of an enormous Fascist plot. For a while the Communist Press of the whole world was flaming with this kind of thing (*Daily Worker*, 21 June, summarizing various Spanish Communist papers):

SPANISH TROTSKYISTS PLOT WITH FRANCO

Following the arrest of a large number of leading Trotskyists in Barcelona and elsewhere . . . there became known, over the weekend, details of one of the most ghastly pieces of espionage ever known in wartime, and the ugliest revelation of Trotskyist treachery to date. . . . Documents in the possession of the police, together with the full confession of no less than 200 persons under arrest, prove, etc. etc.

What these revelations "proved" was that the P.O.U.M. leaders were transmitting military secrets to General Franco by radio, were in touch with Berlin and were acting in collaboration with the secret Fascist organization in Madrid. In addition there were sensational details about secret messages in invisible ink, a mysterious document signed with the letter N. (standing for Nin), and so on and so forth.

But the final upshot was this: six months after the event, as I write, most of the P.O.U.M. leaders are still in jail, but they have never been brought to trial, and the charges of communicating with Franco by radio, etc., have never even been formulated. Had they really been guilty of espionage they would have been tried and shot in a week, as so many Fascist spies had been previously. But not a scrap of evidence was ever produced except the unsupported statements in the Communist Press. As for the two hundred "full confessions," which, if they had existed, would have been enough to convict anybody, they have never been heard of again. They were, in fact, two hundred efforts of somebody's imagination.

More than this, most of the members of the Spanish Government have disclaimed all belief in the charges against the P.O.U.M. Recently the cabinet decided by five to two in favour of releasing anti-Fascist political prisoners; the two dissentients being the Communist ministers. In August an international delegation headed by James Maxton, M.P., went to Spain to inquire into the charges against the P.O.U.M. and the disappearance of Andrés Nin. Prieto, the Minister of National Defence, Irujo, the Minister of Justice, Zugazagoitia, Minister of the Interior, Colonel Ortega, the Procureur-General, Prat García, and others all repudiated any belief in the P.O.U.M. leaders being guilty of espionage. Irujo added that he had been through the dossier of the case, that none of the so-called pieces of evidence would bear examination, and that the document supposed to have been signed by Nin was "valueless" — i.e. a forgery. Prieto considered the P.O.U.M. leaders to be responsible for the May fighting in Barcelona, but dismissed the idea of their being Fascist spies. "What is most grave," he added, "is that the arrest of the P.O.U.M. leaders was not decided upon by the Government, and the police carried out these arrests on their own authority. Those responsible are not the heads of the police, but their entourage, which has been infiltrated by the Communists according to their usual custom." He cited other cases of illegal arrests by the police. Irujo likewise declared that the police had become "quasi-independent" and were in reality under the control of foreign Communist elements. Prieto hinted fairly broadly to the delegation that the Government could not afford to offend the Communist Party while the Russians were supplying arms. When another delegation, headed by John McGovern, M.P., went to Spain in December, they got much the same answers as before, and Zugazagoitia, the Minister of the Interior, repeated

Prieto's hint in even plainer terms. "We have received aid from Russia and have had to permit certain actions which we did not like." As an illustration of the autonomy of the police, it is interesting to learn that even with a signed order from the Director of Prisons and the Minister of Justice, McGovern and the others could not obtain admission to one of the "secret prisons" maintained by the Communist Party in Barcelona.

I think this should be enough to make the matter clear. The accusation of espionage against the P.O.U.M. rested solely upon articles in the Communist Press and the activities of the Communist-controlled secret police. The P.O.U.M. leaders, and hundreds or thousands of their followers, are still in prison, and for six months past the Communist press has continued to clamour for the execution of the "traitors." But Negrín and the others have kept their heads and refused to stage a wholesale massacre of "Trotskyists." Considering the pressure that has been put upon them, it is greatly to their credit that they have done so. Meanwhile, in the face of what I have quoted above, it becomes very difficult to believe that the P.O.U.M. was really a Fascist spying organization, unless one also believes that Maxton, McGovern, Prieto, Irujo, Zugazagoitia, and the rest are all in Fascist pay together.

Finally, as to the charge that the P.O.U.M. was "Trotskyist." This word is now flung about with greater and greater freedom, and it is used in a way that is extremely misleading and is often intended to mislead. It is worth stopping to define it. The word Trotskyist is used to mean three distinct things:

(i) One who, like Trotsky, advocates "world revolution" as against "Socialism in a single country." More loosely, a revolutionary extremist.

(ii) A member of the actual organization of which Trotsky is head.

(iii) A disguised Fascist posing as a revolutionary who acts especially by sabotage in the U.S.S.R., but, in general, by splitting and undermining the Left-wing forces.

In sense (i) the P.O.U.M. could probably be described as Trotskyist. So can the English I.L.P., the German S.A.P., the Left Socialists in France, and so on. But the P.O.U.M. had no connection with Trotsky or the Trotskyist ("Bolshevik-Leninist") organization. When the war broke out the foreign Trotskyists who came to Spain (fifteen or twenty in number) worked at first for the P.O.U.M., as the party nearest to their own viewpoint, but without becoming party-members; later Trotsky ordered his followers to attack the P.O.U.M. policy, and the Trotskyists were purged from the party offices, though a few remained in the militia. Nin, the P.O.U.M. leader after Maurín's capture by the Fascists, was at one time Trotsky's secretary, but had left him some years earlier and formed the P.O.U.M. by the amalgamation of various Opposition Communists with an earlier party, the Workers' and Peasants' Bloc. Nin's one-time association with Trotsky has been used in the Communist Press to show that the P.O.U.M. was really Trotskyist. By the same line of argument it could be shown that the English Communist Party is really a Fascist organization, because of Mr. John Strachey's one-time association with Sir Oswald Mosley.

In sense (ii), the only exactly defined sense of the word, the P.O.U.M. was certainly not Trotskyist. It is important to make this distinction, because it is taken for granted by the majority of Communists that a Trotskyist in sense (ii) is invariably a Trotskyist in sense (iii) — i.e. that the whole Trotskyist organization is simply a Fascist spying-machine. "Trotskyism" only came into public notice in the time of the Russian sabotage trials, and to call a man a Trotskyist is practically equivalent to calling him a murderer, agent provocateur, etc. But at the same time anyone who criticizes Communist policy from a Left-wing standpoint is liable to be denounced as a Trotskyist. Is it then asserted that everyone professing revolutionary extremism is in Fascist pay?

In practice it is or is not, according to local convenience. When Maxton went to Spain with the delegation I have mentioned above, *Verdad, Frente Rojo,* and other Spanish Communist papers instantly denounced him as a "Trotsky-Fascist," spy of the Gestapo and so forth. Yet the English Communists were careful not to repeat this accusation. In the English Communist Press Maxton becomes merely a "reactionary enemy of the working class," which is conveniently vague. The reason, of course, is simply that several sharp lessons have given the English Communist Press a wholesome dread of the law of libel. The fact that the accusation was not repeated in a country where it might have to be proved is sufficient confession that it is a lie.

It may seem that I have discussed the accusations against the P.O.U.M. at greater length than was necessary. Compared with the huge miseries of a civil war, this kind of internecine squabble between parties, with its inevitable injustices and false accusations, may appear trivial. It is not really so. I believe that libels and press-campaigns of this kind, and the habits of mind they indicate, are capable of doing the most deadly damage to the anti-Fascist cause.

Anyone who has given the subject a glance knows that the Communist tactic of dealing with political opponents by means of trumped-up accusations is nothing new. Today the key-word is "Trotsky-Fascist"; yesterday it was "Social-Fascist." It is only six or seven years since the Russian State trials "proved" that the leaders of the Second International, including, for instance, Léon Blum and prominent members of the British Labour Party, were hatching a huge plot for the military invasion of the U.S.S.R. Yet today the French Communists are glad enough to accept Blum as a leader, and the English Communists are raising heaven and earth to get inside the Labour Party. I doubt whether this kind of thing pays, even from a sectarian point of view. And meanwhile there is no possible doubt about the hatred and dissension that the "Trotsky-Fascist" accusation is causing. Rank-and-file Communists everywhere are led away on a senseless witch-hunt after "Trotskyists," and parties of the type of the P.O.U.M. are driven back into the terribly sterile position of being mere anti-Communist parties. There is already the beginning of a dangerous split in the world working-class movement. A few more libels against lifelong Socialists, a few more frame-ups like the charges against the P.O.U.M., and the split may become irreconcilable. The only hope is to keep political controversy on a plane where exhaustive discussion is possible. Between the Communists and those who stand or claim to stand to the Left of them there is a real difference. The Communists hold that Fascism can be beaten by alliance with sections of the capitalist class (the Popular Front); their opponents hold that this manoeuvre simply gives Fascism new breeding-grounds. The question has got to be settled; to make the wrong decision may be to land ourselves in for centuries of semi-slavery. But so long as no argument is produced except a scream of "Trotsky-Fascist!" the discussion cannot even begin. It would be impossible for me, for instance, to debate the rights and wrongs of the Barcelona fighting with a Communist Party member, because no Communist — that is to say, no "good" Communist — could admit that I have given a truthful account of the facts. If he followed his party "line" dutifully he would have to declare that I am lying or, at best, that I am hopelessly mislead and that anyone who glanced at the *Daily Worker* headlines a thousand miles from the scene of events knows more of what was happening in Barcelona than I do. In such circumstances there can be no argument; the necessary minimum of agreement cannot be reached. What purpose is served by saying that men like Maxton are in Fascist pay? Only the purpose of making serious discussion impossible. It is as though in the middle of a chess tournament one competitor should suddenly begin screaming that the other is guilty of arson or bigamy. The point that is really at issue remains untouched. Libel settles nothing.

American Catholic and Protestant Attitudes Towards the Civil War

F. JAY TAYLOR

Professor F. Jay Taylor, currently President of the Louisiana Polytechnic Institute, made the first detailed study of the actions and reactions of the United States towards the Spanish Civil War. His work is based upon a wide variety of sources: Congressional debates, the daily press, journals of opinion, diplomatic dispatches, and the memoirs of leading political, religious, and intellectual figures. Both Protestants and Catholics in the pluralistic United States were probably surprised, and certainly were disturbed, by the extent to which their religious affiliations colored their attitude towards a foreign war. The dilemma was sharpest for the Catholics, whose hierarchy, both in the United States and Europe, supported the Nationalist cause which in turn depended so heavily on the armed intervention of the fascist powers Italy and Germany. The reader should note the unfamiliar presence of religious passion in American public discussion, and the now familiar manner of branding as "communism" any generally leftist government whose program threatens established political, economic, and religious interests.

These pages discuss, in an international context, some of the same problems treated by Brenan and Peers in a Spanish setting. Why did the Spanish Church, fully conscious of world opinion, openly support the Nationalists? Why did the Catholic Church in America espouse the cause of General Franco? Why, also, did many U.S. Catholics roundly refuse to support the Nationalists? Why were American Protestants so disturbed by Church support of Franco? And what were the international implications for the Church of its stand in the Spanish Civil War?

THE PRECARIOUS POSITION of the Catholic Church in Spain was an issue which for many people throughout the world transcended the political implications of the Spanish Civil War. Pope Pius XI openly sympathized with the Spanish Nationalists as it was his belief that the Loyalists were attempting to destroy the Church and convert Spain into a communistic state. The Pope declared that of all the perils which confronted human society, "the first, the greatest and now the general peril, is certainly communism in all its forms and degrees." Accordingly, Pius XI charged that spreading Bolshevist propaganda in Europe caused the Spanish Civil War:

Satanic preparation has relighted — and that more fiercely — in neighboring Spain that hatred and savage persecution which have been confessedly reserved for the Catholic Church and Catholic religion as being the one real obstacle.

Our benediction, above any political and mundane consideration, goes in a special manner to all those who assume the difficult and dangerous task of defending and restoring the rights to honor God and religion.

In May 1938 the Pope blessed General Franco, stating, "We send from our hearts the apostolic blessing, propitiator of divine favors"; and in April 1939, when the Nationalist army emerged victorious, the Pope telegraphed Franco: "Lifting up our heart

From F. Jay Taylor, *The United States and the Spanish Civil War* (New York, 1956), pp. 143–159. Reprinted by permission of Twayne Publishers, Inc.

to God, we give sincere thanks with your Excellency for Spain's Catholic victory." Nor did Ambassador Bowers believe that the Pope was neutral in the Spanish struggle. In a letter to President Roosevelt the Ambassador wrote that he was amused at the suggestion of Camille Chautemps, the French Premier, that the Pope was neutral in his feelings. Bowers declared: "He is just as neutral as he was in the case of Abyssinia. He is a very loyal Italian always. He has been favorable to the fascist cause in Spain, supported by 70,000 of Mussolini's army, throughout."

In the United States a large majority of the supporters of General Franco were Catholics. This seemed to indicate that religion was the chief factor in determining their attitude. Shortly after the outbreak of the Spanish Civil War the *Catholic World* published an article which reflected the views already prevalent among many Catholics in this country. This article, reprinted from the *Catholic Herald* of London, described the Madrid Government as communistic and stated that it was evident that the Soviet Union would attempt to interfere in the Spanish War. "Under these circumstances the anti-communist governments may reasonably hesitate to pledge themselves for an indefinite period of nonintervention." Although communism was an enemy of the Church, this writer sounded an apologetic note when he stated that Catholics could not view with satisfaction the dependence of Catholic institutions and culture on the protection of the anti-Communist dictators or the leaders of the military revolt in Spain. It was only an accident, he said, that Catholics and dictators had the same enemy — communism. In a Communist dictatorship hostility to Catholic life is complete and only anti-Communist dictators afforded a military shield for the Church against communism.

The editors of the *Catholic World* were much more vigorous in the denunciation of the Loyalist Government than had been the writer in the *Herald*. They charged that the Madrid regime was "an anti-clerical government that has unleashed its fury against the Church." The editors asserted that priests and nuns were killed while all the churches, convents, monasteries, religious schools, and private chapels in Barcelona had gone up in flames. Thus in view of this open hostility to Catholicism, Catholics must unite to save the Church from its avowed enemies who were then in control of the Government. The *Tidings,* official organ of the Los Angeles Archdiocese, warned that the Spanish Popular Front Government would drive the United States into war and the world would be endangered by the spread of communism.

Other Catholics visited Spain and brought back news of "what is really happening" in that war-torn country. Rev. Karl J. Alter, Bishop of Toledo (Ohio), said that wherever he went, "Americans, including many non-Catholics, approached him and urged him to tell the American people . . . the truth about Nationalist Spain." That the struggle was "really . . . a war to save religion, morality and civilization itself." In describing conditions in Toledo (Spain) Bishop Alter stated that

only five of the original 28 canons of the Cathedral are still alive, the rest have been slain by the Reds; from the Cathedral and other churches valuable manuscripts, chalices, ciboria, monstrances, etc., have been stolen by the Reds; Red airplanes have daily dropped explosives on towns of no military value; churches, altars, shrines, etc., have been needlessly and ruthlessly destroyed, bodies exhumed and valuables on the corpses removed . . . side altars of the Church were hacked and smashed, the main altar had been set afire, and that in an adjoining convent crypts had been opened and the bodies of nuns dragged out and left on the floor.

Regarding his own feelings on the Spanish issue the Bishop told his congregation that

I am not neutral. I don't want to be neutral. I want to be fair, objective and intelligently honest. According to the facts, there is only one side in Spain that can be intelligently and conscientiously approved — and that is

Nationalist Spain. The other side is guilty of crimes that will seem fantastic when the American people learn of them.

Certain Protestant groups were distressed by the antagonism exhibited by the Catholics toward the Spanish Republican Government. In their eyes support for Franco meant support for Hitler and Mussolini; thus the Catholic Church in America became the object of much criticism. A large number of Protestants saw the strife in Spain as a struggle between fascism and democracy and it was difficult for them to understand the position taken by most Catholics. Nor was it felt that the Catholics were being wholly fair in their interpretation of events in Spain. The *Christian Century* commented that

to a great extent the church [Catholic] has thrown the weight of its influence upon the side of Franco and the insurgents. Italian troops have gone into the war with banners blessed by the church. It has played its part in representing the conflict as one between atheistic bolshevism and the crusading forces of Christianity. It has striven to create the impression that the loyalists were murderous ruffians whose most characteristic activities were desecrating altars, slaughtering priests and raping nuns, while the rebels and their invading allies were practically advancing on their knees.

Advance, an organ of the Congregational Church, charged that all Catholics who supported the Loyalist Government were severely censured by the Catholic hierarchy. The editors warned the Catholics, however, that such a position was shortsighted and likely to drive many liberals away from the Church. A prominent religious writer [Reinhold Niebuhr] declared that the attitude of the Catholic Church in regard to Spain was the "height of spiritual arrogance," and that the Church was "too blind to see that it is defending a corrupt and unjust civilization against a rising passion for justice."

One of the most formidable controversies of the Spanish War developed between Protestants and Catholics in the United States over a joint pastoral letter prepared by the Catholic hierarchy in Spain which justified the revolt against the Spanish Government. The Spanish prelates stated that "false opinion created abroad, particularly by a certain group of Spanish Catholics [the Basque Autonomous Government] necessitated the letter." There were five principal points in the argument of the Spanish bishops: (1) The Church did not want the war in Spain although "thousands of her sons have taken arms on their personal responsibility to save the principles of religion and Christian justice." (2) Since the Spanish Republic was proclaimed in 1931 the legislative and executive power in Spain had changed Spanish history in a manner contrary to the needs of the national spirit. (3) The elections of February 1936 were unjust. Although the Right and Center parties received 500,000 more votes than the parties of the Left, the former group elected 118 fewer deputies because of the arbitrary annulment of votes in all the provinces. (4) The Communist International had armed a revolutionary Spanish militia so that Spain was virtually an armed camp when the war broke out. (5) The civil war was legitimate because

five years of continued outrages of Spanish subjects in the religious and social fields had endangered the very existence of public welfare and had produced enormous spiritual unrest among the Spanish people; and because when the legal means were exhausted the idea entered the national conscience that there was no other recourse except force to maintain order and peace. Also because interests opposed to legitimate authority had decided to overthrow the constituted order and establish communism through violence. Finally, because, through the fatal logic of facts, Spain had only this alternative: either to perish under the precipitate assault of destructive communism, already prepared and decreed, as has happened in the area where the Nationalist Government has not triumphed, or to attempt with titanic force to get rid of his frightful enemy and save the fundamental principles of our social life and national characteristics.

Four conclusions were drawn by the prelates: (1) "The Church could not remain indifferent in a fight, in which on one side, God was renounced, while on the other side, notwithstanding human defects, the fight was for the preservation of the old Spain and Christian spirit." (2) The Church, however, "does not associate herself with acts, tendencies, and intentions that figure in the noble physiognomy of the Nationalist movement." (3) The civil-military uprising "deepens in the people's consciousness two roots; one of patriotism, and the other of religious sentiment." (4) There is no other hope that Spain may again have justice and peace except through the Nationalist movement.

The letter from Spain provoked a heated exchange of statements by Protestant and Catholic leaders in this country. In a letter prepared by Dr. Guy Emery Shipler, editor of the *Churchman,* an independent Episcopal paper, and signed by 150 Protestant clergymen, educators, and laymen, the Spanish hierarchy was denounced for its stand. The Protestants stated that it was hard to believe that the letter had been written in the twentieth century, and charged that by the opinions expressed the Catholic hierarchy in Spain demonstrated their "open hostility toward the popular principles of freedom of worship and separation of church and state." They characterized as "alarming" the bishops' "attempt to justify a military rebellion against a legally elected government." In so doing, they asserted, the hierarchy acted as "the apologists for reaction and fascism." The letter continued: "Certainly the hierarchy can hardly expect to gain sympathy there, either for itself or for the Catholic religion with a declaration that treats with contempt principles that are the precious heritage of the American people." The Protestants were also disturbed by the fact that "no leaders of the Catholic Church in America have raised their voice in repudiation of the position taken by the Spanish hierarchy," and added that "they too seem to have given their blessing to General Franco and his Fascist allies." They declared that the pastoral letter approved of resort to violence, rejected not only the Popular Front Government of Spain, but also democratic institutions and the Spanish Republic itself. "It is clear," they maintained, "that the Spanish conflict is between the forces of democracy and social progress, on the one hand, and the forces of special privilege, and their Fascist allies on the other." Conceding that there had been excesses on the Loyalist side, the letter asserted that the Madrid regime had made every effort to prevent such occurrences, while on the Insurgent side Franco had encouraged violence. The Protestants stated that the Spanish hierarchy was indifferent to the actual facts of brutality and atrocities on the Rebel side. They claimed that priests and nuns had been murdered within Nationalist territory, and the Protestant missions had been destroyed by the Insurgents.

This document led to an immediate response by American Catholics. The Reverend Francis X. Talbot, editor of the Jesuit weekly, *America,* declared that the Protestants signing the letter were "misinformed of the facts" and were voicing opinions that had long been discredited. The open letter "neither establishes the point that it proposes nor engenders faith in the honesty of its authors or signatories." Father Talbot then declared that the

> Protestant Christians of the United States, if they are to remain faithful to the principles of Christ, must repudiate the anti-Christ propaganda and practices of the Loyalist government, composed as it is of Communists, anarchists, syndicalists, and atheistic groups in Spain. By such an open letter published over their signatures they foster atheism and agnosticism.

A similar expression was voiced by Reverend John J. O'Conner, acting managing editor of the *Commonweal,* who said that "if the distinguished gentlemen still believe that the struggle in Spain 'is between the forces of democracy and social progress on the one hand and the forces of special privilege and their Fascist allies on the other,' we can only express our regret that they have been so completely and so thoroughly hoodwinked." Msgr. Michael J. Ready, General Secretary of the National Catholic Welfare Conference, commented that he could "only express astonishment that so large a number of intelligent and presumably fair-minded American Protestants, so far removed from the scene of the conflict and the sources of true information, could be stampeded into so harsh and hostile a diatribe against the harassed and suffering bishops of Spain."

Ten days after the open letter of the Protestants was published 175 Catholics officially replied that the letter "misrepresented the facts and issues in Spain." The Catholic statement charged the existence of a "campaign of misrepresentation, errors and deliberate lies" against the Insurgents and challenged the Protestants to say whether they accepted and approved of a regime "which has carried on a ruthless persecution of the Christian religion since February 1936." The statement asserted that Catholics who supported Franco did so as private citizens and not as members of the Church. It was argued that the Communists seized power and attempted to institute a "Soviet Dictatorship," and were violating civil rights in Spain before the Army rose in revolt. The Catholic spokesmen stated that the reason Catholics supported the insurrection was to "save themselves from destruction and annihilation, not only as Catholics but as citizens." Charges of Insurgent atrocities were denied while it was maintained that the Communists had burned "all" the Catholic churches in the area they controlled, had destroyed "all" religious objects, and had "massacred virtually all priests in an attempt to destroy the Catholic religion." In conclusion the statement asserted that

the Madrid Government then ruling Spain did not represent the will of the people, as two thirds of the Spaniards had "freely and enthusiastically acclaimed loyalty and allegiance to General Franco."

In discussing the controversy over the Spanish prelates' letter, the editors of the *Nation* commented that American Catholics were placed in a very embarrassing position as "the savage tactics of the Christian Knight [Franco], his employment of Moors, and his close association with the neopagan, Catholic-baiting followers of Hitler has spread much doubt among the faithful." They added that the Catholics must speak out or accept fascism as the protector of the faith. The editors of the *New Republic* described the pastoral letter of the Spaniards as a "boomerang," and claimed that it was not well received by Catholics throughout the world. James T. Shotwell, Professor of History at Columbia University, in a letter to the *New York Times,* declared that the Spanish bishops have been blind to the social changes that have occurred in Spain which were unrelated to communism. It was Shotwell's belief that the "prelates have neither proved their case against their enemies nor justified their own." In an effort to ameliorate the controversy Bishop Robert L. Paddock stated that he had signed the letter written by the Protestants, but did so "with no malice or intent to misrepresent, and certainly with no unfriendliness to the Roman Catholics in this country." He suggested that at least in matters concerning religion, "may we avoid calling each other names and feel and show a brotherly spirit."

On October 19, 1937, an open invitation was extended by Spanish Ambassador de los Ríos for a mixed commission representing both Catholic and Protestant groups to go to Spain and visit both sides in order that "the whole question could be objectively clarified." Bishop Paddock, speaking as a member of the Protestant group, accepted the invitation, but no official Catholic reply was made. In February

1939 a second invitation was extended by the Ambassador to prominent American Catholics to visit Loyalist Spain. No Catholics accepted this offer and Archbishop Michael Joseph Curley declined with the statement: "I guess he would have me come over wearing my clerical collar — and get murdered. . . . Any word or action of the Spanish Loyalist Government friendly to the Church . . . must be taken as a sign of fraud, or of self-deception, or of the repudiation of its principles."

There were many Catholics in the United States who felt that it was their religious duty to defend publicly General Franco and the "holy cause" for which he was fighting. There is evidence which would seem to indicate that members of the Church sometimes acted as pressure groups to influence American opinion and official policy toward the Spanish Civil War. J. David Stern was threatened with a Catholic boycott for printing in the *Philadelphia Record* an editorial supporting the Popular Front Government in Spain, and better relations were not restored with Catholic leaders until a second editorial was printed correcting some of the impressions created by the first. Michael Williams, editor of the *Commonweal*, felt so strongly about the alleged distortion of facts printed in the *Record* concerning the Spanish conflict that he challenged Stern to a public debate on the subject. The *New Orleans Times-Picayune*, apparently pro-Loyalist in its sympathies, was warned by the editors of *Catholic Action of the South*:

No intelligently directed newspaper wants to offend the majority of its readers . . . because we feel that the *Times-Picayune* considers the goodwill of the Catholics in its field to be of value to its business, hence would not attempt, even if they were not in sympathy with Catholic feelings, to consistently carry headlines and phraseology describing happenings in Spain in a manner that is most offensive to Catholics and to all liberty loving citizens.

It was suggested that the *Times-Picayune* "check up on its information and instruct its headline writers and news story writers at least to consider the feelings of most of the newspaper's readers."

Another writer reported that Catholic students in St. Louis wrote hundreds of letters to the *St. Louis Post-Dispatch* because of its editorial stand on Spain. Lawrence Fernsworth, who was a Catholic and one of the Spanish correspondents for the *New York Times*, charged in a public lecture that "political forces in the Roman Catholic Church both here and abroad brought constant pressure on him to distort his reporting from Loyalist territory during the Spanish War." He stated that Father Talbot, editor of the Jesuit weekly, *America*, warned him that, as a Catholic, it was his duty to express his opinions to the hierarchy in Spain before writing his dispatches.

Nor were Catholic pressure tactics confined to the press; they extended to the motion picture industry as well. The Walter Wanger film, "Blockade," which was a sermon against the slaughter of noncombatants in the Spanish Civil War, created much controversy. Although the producer prefaced the film with a statement that it was not intended as propaganda for either side in Spain, even the most casual observer could not fail to identify the carefully unspecified enemy as the forces of General Franco bombing cities, sinking food ships, and destroying hospitals. The Catholic Church launched a drive against the film on the ground that it presented a case for the "Communists" in Spain and was therefore atheistic. The National Legion of Decency, which had behind it the authority of the Catholic Church, did not specifically ban the picture but placed it in a special category with the observation that "many people will regard this picture as containing foreign political propaganda in favor of one side in the present unfortunate struggle in Spain." Pressure was exerted on the Catholic manager of Radio City Music Hall to prevent him from exhibiting the film; in Boston the City Council adopted a resolution condemning the film, but later the mayor permitted its showing with two deletions; the commissioner of licenses in Providence, Rhode Island, banned the picture on a second run after it had already made one appearance; and the Fox West Coast Theater chain refused to exhibit the film, which — in view of the movie's financial success elsewhere — was apparently the result of outside pressure.

"Blockade" was also denounced in the Catholic press. The *Catholic News* predicted that it would "stir up prejudice, bad feeling, and contention," while the *Brooklyn Tablet* demanded "Blockade 'Blockade.'" The Jesuit weekly, *America,* declared that the picture was significant because it was "the first picture to raise the question of propaganda issuing from Leftist brains in Hollywood." Joseph Lamb, deputy of the New York Council, Knights of Columbus, denounced the movie as "subtle pro-Loyalist propaganda"; while Martin Carmody, Supreme Knight of Columbus, speaking for the 500,000 members of his organization, declared that the film was historically false and intellectually dishonest. On the other hand the *Nation, New Masses,* the *American Guardian,* and other liberal and leftist publications urged their readers to crown "Blockade" with "box office success." There were also several other motion pictures about the war in Spain which were condemned by many Catholics. The Pennsylvania censor board banned the film, "Spain in Flames," from the theaters of that state on the grounds that the picture was recruiting propaganda for the Loyalists, while the documentary film, "Spanish Earth," received similar treatment in Detroit.

It is interesting to note, however, that the political views of the Catholic hierarchy were not binding on all Catholics. Many well-known Catholics such as Kathleen Norris, Westbrook Pegler, George M. Schuster, Shaemas O'Sheel, Lawrence Fernsworth, and millions of lesser known individuals, particularly those in trade unions, were either opposed to Franco or actively pro-Loyalist. Unpublished polls of the American Institute of Public Opinion disclosed that despite hierarchy pressure only four out of ten Catholics were sympathetic with the Franco regime. In observing the Gallup reports which revealed that 76 per cent of those Americans expressing an opinion favored the Loyalists, the editors of *Catholic Action* remarked that "we cannot escape the deeply disturbing fact that . . . some Catholics — and in numbers to have real significance — voted . . . for the Spanish 'Loyalists.'"

Many Catholics feared that a possible identification of fascism with Catholicism in Spain might have very unfortunate effects on Catholicism in all democratic countries. One Catholic writer denounced the hierarchy for its support of the Franco Government and fascism, pointing out that the political views of the bishops or even the Pope were not binding upon individual Catholics. This writer stated that non-Catholics should not make the mistake of assuming that all Catholics have "lined up with Franco at the snap of the ecclesiastical whip," and added that Catholics "need to be told that they are not repudiating the Church of Christ when they repudiate politically the hierarchy." Another Catholic, the syndicated columnist Westbrook Pegler, had his column dropped by many regular subscribers, including the *New York World-Telegram,* when he told his readers that he could not "see why the working class Catholics are expected to be indignant against the government side in Spain. . . . If I were a Spaniard who had seen Franco's missionary work among the children I might see him in hell but never in the Church." George M. Schuster apologized for his Church and stated that the reason Catholics in the United States defended Franco was because of "minorityitis." He explained that Catholics felt very insecure in their position and when the bulk of American opinion supported the Loyalists, "Catholic resentment rose up against deeply ingrained non-Catholic instinct." Then, taking a middle course, Schuster said that on a recent tour of Europe he found but few who sympathized with either side "but the majority believed that Spain would recover only if some way were found of arbitrating the dispute."

Perhaps the most spectacular indictment of the Church's attitude toward the Spanish Civil War was made by an alleged Catholic priest who wrote under the pen name of Peter Whiffin. He asserted that many Catholics tried to blame everything antireligious on Russian communism, but "that's just trying to pass the buck." When a Cardinal, said the priest, blamed the Spanish conflict on sixty Russians attempting to spread the Communist doctrine, then, that Cardinal

succeeds only in making a most damning indictment of the Spanish Church and clergy. For, if 60 Russians in three years could overturn the entire Spanish Church, after all her centuries of domination, with all her thousands of priests and religious, with all her millions of Catholics, and with all her power and organization and wealth — and overturn her so completely that she needed a counter-revolution and thousands of black soldiers and the substantial help of Italy and Germany to put her back on her feet — then surely there must be something very foul about the Spanish Church. There is no other explanation.

Father Whiffin was subjected to extreme criticism by many Catholics and the Catholic press, so much that several months later in a paid advertisement the priest altered many of his views. He did not, however, retract his indictment of the Catholic hierarchy and its attitude toward the Spanish Civil War.

The Catholic position regarding the Spanish conflict was further weakened when in June 1938 a very influential Catholic journal reversed its stand regarding the war in Spain. The *Commonweal*, after a change of editors, adopted an impartial attitude between the two opposing sides and asked that its readers do likewise. In an editorial defending this new policy, the editors stated that it was hard to learn the truth of what had happened in Spain. Information from both sides had been so generally characterized by propaganda that the American people did not have sufficient knowledge of the whole situation. They asserted that Spain had to choose between two governments "whose characters were mixed and impossible to know." One side permitted the murder of priests and nuns and maintained a close alliance with Russia; the other side bombed defenseless cities, held totalitarian views, and were allied with Fascist nations. The only duty of Americans, the *Commonweal* declared was to alleviate distress and suffering on both sides while working for peace. The editorial stated that the wisest policy for Americans was "positive impartiality" with sanity of judgment toward both sides.

Michael Williams, the former editor, wrote an article the same week which took issue with the new editorial policy, asserting that a Franco victory would be beneficial to the cause of Christian civilization. Although admitting uncertainty in the news, he stated that all reports from Spain were not propaganda, and the fact was not to be denied that the Popular Front Government was attempting to destroy the Catholic Church.

Three weeks later the editors of the *Commonweal* reviewed the sentiment that had been expressed concerning their revised attitude regarding Spain. They stated that there was no overwhelming support either for or against the new policy. The letters they had received were rather equally divided in sentiment and raised issues which could be listed under three separate categories. First, there was the problem of evidence. The readers inquired if the editors were taking a proper or improper attitude toward the evidence available. Secondly, they were asked if all Catholics were not obliged to support Franco. Finally, the question of "positive neutrality" was raised, what it was and what it meant for Americans. Editorial comment in the Catholic press was generally critical. The Jesuit publications, *America* and *Blackfriars,* strongly criticized the attitude of the *Commonweal* and condemned the Loyalist activities against the Church. The *New World,* official organ of the Chicago Archdiocese, agreed that war was a strong possibility in Europe and that America should maintain a policy of strict neutrality, but expressed sympathy for the Catholic forces in Spain fighting communism. The *Catholic Worker* was one Catholic journal, however, that applauded the new policy of the *Commonweal.* The *Worker* was unique among Catholic papers. It was published in New York and to its 75,000 subscribers preached a sort of "Catholic communism," but rejected violence, class war, revolution, and international war. Throughout the course of the Spanish War the editors advocated a policy of sympathy and support for the Loyalist regime in Spain.

Although a majority of the people in the United States reviewed events across the Atlantic as not involving them directly, there were many Catholics who continued to be agitated over incidents concerning the Spanish conflict. One such incident occurred in January 1938 when sixty members of Congress sent a telegram of congratulations to the Loyalist Cortes meeting in Valencia:

We, the undersigned Members of the Congress of the United States, are happy to send our greetings and good wishes to the Spanish Parliament on the occasion of its regular session convened in accordance with the provisions of the Constitution of 1931. For you to meet again in the face of trying and tragic circumstances of the present demonstrates that the Spanish people and their representatives stand firm in their faith in democratic government.
We, who cherish freedom and democracy above all else, realize the significance of your heroic and determined fight to save democratic institutions in your country from its enemies both within and without Spain. Your struggle sets a stirring example to all democratic peoples. As members of one democratically elected parliament to another, we salute you.

Certain Catholic leaders immediately condemned the message. Monsignor Michael J. Ready, Chairman of the National Catholic Welfare Conference, asserted that it was incredible "to believe that the duly elected representatives of our American democracy, sworn to uphold the right of religious liberty, could place themselves on record as sympathetic with a government which has absolutely proscribed the exercise of religion in the territory which it governs." Bishop James E. Walsh declared that he was "amazed" at the message sent to a Communist government that was responsible for "Catholic massacres," while the National Catholic Alumni Federation issued a public statement strongly criticizing the signers of the telegram. This feeling was reflected on the local level when, for example, the Lafayette (Louisiana) Diocesan Council of Catholic Women wrote Senator Allen J. Ellender (D-Louisiana) that they were "deeply grieved as Christians and Americans at the report of your having signed the greeting"; and the Holy Name Society of Holy Ghost Parish (Hammond, Louisiana) objected to Ellender's "sympathizing and encouraging a government which has shown itself to be little more than a puppet of Communist Russia."

On February 10, 1938, an N. C. W. C. dispatch announced: "Sixty Congressmen Turn Out to be 17; 'Message' Backfires on Red Publicists." One of the news agency's staff correspondents made a canvass of the sixty Senators and Representatives who had signed the message and disclosed that four retracted their endorsement of the document, twenty-six did not intend to express sympathy with the Loyalist Government but signed the message only as a "Greeting to Democracy," four had nothing to say on the subject, seventeen declared that they had meant to express sympathy to the Spanish Republican Government, while the comments of five of the signers were listed as unclassified. The National Catholic Welfare Conference announced that this investigation proved: (1) That the message was not in the slightest degree spontaneous with the Congressmen, but was promoted by outsiders sympathetic to "leftist" Spain. (2) That four Senators retracted their signatures. (3) That half of the signers did not mean by their signatures to favor the Barcelona Government. (4) That actually less than a third were definitely willing to say that they meant their endorsement to express sympathy with the Loyalist regime. (5) That some of the signers charged trickery was used to obtain their signatures.

Representative Fred Hildebrandt (D-South Dakota) explained that many groups in his constituency had called for an explanation of his motives in signing a message of greeting to the Spanish Parliament, the assumption being that he had publicly allied himself with one of the opposing factions in Spain. Hildebrandt stated that he was sorry this "innocent gesture" of greeting was diverted to propaganda uses. "I am sympathetic to the feeling of shock suffered by those religious groups in this country who, by the universality of their creed, have more than an academic interest in the outcome of the Spanish war." The Congressman charged that a second paragraph was later added to the document that he had signed since he "would not knowingly lend whatever prestige my name conveys to one belligerent group as against another, whether it be in Spain, Ethiopia, or China."

Representative Burdick (R-North Dakota) likewise announced that he had made a serious mistake in signing the petition. Burdick declared that he had signed the message because he felt that a Fascist regime was attempting to overthrow a democratic government, but that one thousand letters had arrived from his home state expressing "surprise and sadness" that he had signed the document. The Congressman stated that the main argument expressed in the letters written to him was that the revolution in Spain was a religious upheaval and that the Barcelona Government had attempted to destroy the Catholic religion. Burdick declared that since he was not acquainted with the actual conditions in Spain, and since he did not wish to be a party to a religious controversy, "I must, in good conscience, say I made a mistake and withdraw my endorsement." Similar action was taken by Senator Prentiss Brown (D-Michigan) and Senator Clyde Herring (D-Iowa).

Another incident that aroused considerable agitation among certain Catholic groups was the plan announced by a group of American liberals to form a Board of Guardians for Basque Refugee Children and bring five hundred young Basques to the United States for the duration of the Spanish Civil War. Leaders of the movement, Gardner Jackson, Chairman of the American Friends of Spanish Democracy, New York Representative Caroline O'Day, President Mary Emma Woolley of Mt. Holyoke College, Professor James T. Shotwell of Columbia University, and Dr. Frank Bohn, Secretary of the American Board of Guardians of Basque Children, described the plight of these young victims of war and stated that offers had been received from 2,700 American homes to care for the children. The Spanish Chargé d'Affaires informed Under Secretary of State Welles that a group of Spanish Basques who owned a large Mexican hat factory in St. Louis had made known their desire to care for some of the children should they be permitted to enter the United States. Mrs. Eleanor Roosevelt was also very interested in the welfare of these children and at her insistence Ambassador Bowers was made chairman of a committee to help provide for their relief.

In the United States Catholic reaction was very strong in opposition. Even though predominantly Catholic, the Basque people had vigorously supported the Republican Government and had caused the American Catholics no little concern in explaining the alliance between the atheistic "Reds" and Catholic Basques. Cardinal

O'Connell denounced the "ill advised plan" because "other means of relief so readily suggest themselves." Representative John W. McCormack (D-Massachusetts) saw the plan as a smoke-screen for Red propaganda and complained that Basque children previously sent to England and other countries had not necessarily been placed in Catholic homes. McCormack also wrote to President Roosevelt asking to see him concerning the matter. The Secretary of the Massachusetts State Council of the Knights of Columbus likewise wrote to President Roosevelt that "this rash and foolish plan is a real danger to the established neutrality policy of this nation. The unfortunate war victims . . . might easily be used for propaganda purposes by groups actively seeking sympathy for the Communist-Socialist regime of the Madrid-Valencia government." A smilar letter was written to the President by Joseph A. Callahan, High Chief Ranger, Massachusetts Catholic Order of Foresters, who claimed that the childen should be sent to France or other countries closer to their home.

President Roosevelt was influenced, however, probably by Ambassador Bowers and Mrs. Roosevelt, to consult the State Department concerning the possibility of allowing these children to enter the United States for the duration of the Spanish strife. Under Secretary Welles wrote Marvin McIntyre (the President's personal secretary) that the question of permitting the Basque children entrance into the United States was one for the Secretary of Labor to decide. Welles stated that it was his personal view that they should not be brought to this country but should be taken to some country nearer their parents. In any event, despite considerable planning and several public announcements by the American Board of Guardians for Basque Refugee Children, none were ever brought to the United States.

That the succor of children who were the innocent victims of internecine civil war should have become the subject of heated controversy in the United States gives a measure of the temperature of the heated religious controversy engendered by the Spanish conflict.

General Franco Balances Internal Factions and Italo-German Pressures in Nationalist Spain

STANLEY PAYNE

During the Civil War General Francisco Franco served not only as supreme military commander of Nationalist Spain, but also as its political chieftain. Nationalist Spain, though more orderly and outwardly more unified than Republican Spain, nevertheless included many political groupings which were bitterly at odds with each other. The Falange looked to the Italian fascist model, but also included anticlerical and anticapitalist factions. The monarchists were divided between those loyal to the Bourbon line of the exiled King Alfonso XIII and those loyal to the Carlist Pretender. The Italian dictator Mussolini and several German diplomats concerned themselves with the domestic government of Nationalist Spain. In the present selection, Professor Stanley Payne, a leading scholar on the history of the Falange, shows the skill with which Franco balanced the contending forces around him.

The student will want to bear in mind the following questions: What were the differences between Carlist and Falangist aims? Did these aims relate primarily to domestic or international affairs? To what extent did Italy and Germany attempt to influence the domestic politics of Nationalist Spain? Referring to the preceding *Survey* selections, what comparisons can be made as to the degree of foreign influence over domestic affairs in Republican and Nationalist Spain during 1938?

FRANCO AND SERRANO SÚÑER displayed extraordinary skill in balancing off the various incompatible and contradictory elements wedged into the FET [Falange Española Tradicionalista]. The party itself soon became hopelessly faction-ridden, which was just what the dictator wanted. No one really knew where the Caudillo [chieftain, i.e., Franco] stood on the long political spectrum reaching from national syndicalist revolution to clerical reaction. The German ambassador noted:

[Franco] has very cleverly succeeded, with the advice of his brother-in-law, . . . in not making enemies of any of the parties represented in the Unity Party that were previously independent and hostile to one another, . . . but, on the other hand, also in not favoring any one of them that might thus grow too

strong. . . . It is therefore comprehensible that, depending on the party allegiance of the person concerned, one is just as apt to hear the opinion in Spain that "Franco is entirely a creature of the Falange," as that "Franco has sold himself completely to the reaction," or "Franco is a proven monarchist," or "he is completely under the influence of the Church."

Serrano Súñer bore the brunt of the enmity aroused by the new political alignment of 1937. His first and bitterest opponents were not Falangists but monarchists, who realized that with the unification he was trying to lay the basis for a corporative, authoritarian, nonmonarchical state. This created an enormous, seemingly insuperable, obstacle to their plans for a restoration. They launched an extensive

Reprinted from *Falange: A History of Spanish Fascism* by Stanley Payne with the permission of the publishers, Stanford University Press, pp. 179–184, 191–198. © 1961 by the Board of Trustees of the Leland Stanford Junior University.

101

whispering campaign against Franco's evil genius, the *cuñadísimo*.[1]

In his *ABC* interview of July 19, Franco had already rolled out what was to become his standard line for monarchists:

If the time for a Restoration should arrive, the new Monarchy would of course have to be very different from the one which fell on April 14, 1931: different in its content and — though it may grieve many, we must obey reality — even in the person who incarnates it. . . . [That person] ought to have the character of a pacifier and ought not to be numbered among the conquerors.

In short, everything was to be postponed indefinitely. There was no reason to hide the fact that the military dictatorship would be necessary for some time after the war was over. Franco ended with the comforting statement that the aristocracy had made great sacrifices and had shown up well in the war, as if to say that this glory and their personal perquisites should be enough for them.

For his part, Serrano Súñer declared to all that his only goals were "to help establish *effectively* the political *jefatura* [uncontested leadership] of Franco, to save and realize the political thought of José Antonio, and to contribute to establishing the National Movement in a juridical regime, that is, to institute a State of Law." A Falange pedigree was quickly built up for Serrano. His dealings with José Antonio were inflated and noised about, in preparation for greater things to come. When the first regular Franco cabinet was set up on January 30, 1938, the *cuñadísimo* became Minister of the Interior and *Jefe Nacional* of Press and Propaganda for the FET. Serrano now ran internal Nationalist politics.

After the new government list was announced, a howl went up from the *camisas viejas*[2] over the appointment of General Gómez Jordana as Foreign Minister. Jordana was a monarchist and had a reputation as an Anglophile. He would be likely to countenance what Falangists termed the "crime of Gibraltar" and to work for a Bourbon restoration. Furthermore, he was not overly fond of the fascist governments admired by most Falangists.

The old guard was soon given compensation for this affront. Since Serrano, the party's nominal Press and Propaganda Chief, was also head of the Ministry of the Interior, this meant that the Falange propaganda machine could now control the official propaganda of the state. This opened the way for the first of Franco's many compromises. In return for accepting a cabinet packed with conservatives and monarchists, the *camisas viejas* would be allowed to control government rhetoric. As Subsecretaries of Press and of Propaganda for the FET, two young protégés of Serrano, both super-Falangists, were chosen. They were, respectively, Antonio Tóvar and Dionisio Ridruejo.

Ridruejo, only twenty-five years old, set out to establish a "totalitarian" propaganda machine, and the quasi-revolutionary line of the Falange enjoyed a tight monopoly of information outlets. Young Dionisio was soon nicknamed "the Spanish Goebbels" — a strained analogy, based only on the diminutive physical stature of the two men. Dionisio was the most eloquent speaker in the party since José Antonio, and he strove to maintain the vanished *Jefe's* tone of "poetic fascism."

It was evident throughout the first half of 1938 that each temporary military crisis was likely to bring a recrudescence of political differences. As the war dragged on without a clear end in sight, the political malaise deepened. General Juan Yagüe, the "Falange General," grew very tired of the

---

[1] *Cuñado* means brother-in-law, and the suffix *ísimo* indicates the superlative. Hence a sarcastic reference to the influence of Serrano Súñer. [Editor's note.]

[2] Literally "old shirts," half affectionate, half scornful name for the original followers of the martyred founder of the Falange, José Antonio Primo de Rivera. [Editor's note.]

war and the political dealings of the Cuartel General. The calculated cruelty and premeditated hatred of the Civil War disgusted him. He saw few signs of a "new Spain" emerging from the political intrigue around Salamanca. Yagüe was so embittered that during a speech on the first anniversary of the unification he lashed out publicly against the actions of the Caudillo's clique. According to von Stohrer, the German ambassador,

In particular it was felt that the parts of his [Yagüe's] speech in which he gave free recognition to the bravery of the Red Spanish opponents, defended the political prisoners — both the Reds and the "Blues" (Falangists), who were arrested because of too much political zeal — and severely attacked the partiality of the administration of justice, went beyond his authority and represented a lack of discipline; the answer was his recall from command, at least temporarily.

In a major speech at Zaragoza, given on the same day as Yagüe's address, Franco strongly denounced all murmurers and dissenters:

Efforts to infiltrate the cadres of our organizations multiplied; an attempt was made to sow rivalry and division in our ranks; secret orders were given in order to produce lassitude and fatigue. An effort was made to undermine the prestige of our highest authorities by exploiting petty complaints and ambitions.

These are they who want to sound an alarm to capital with the phantasm of demagogic reforms. . . .

Therefore Spain's constant enemies will not cease in their attempt to destroy our unity, as they did even after the decree of unification, speculating at times with the glorious name of José Antonio, founder and martyr of the Falange. . . .

The German ambassador reported that forty per cent of the civilian population in rebel territory were still considered politically unreliable, and were held in place only by the government's policy of ruthless reprisals. All of the more responsible elements in the Franco government were becoming depressed by the sea of blood flowing from the savage police repression intended to guarantee the "internal security" of the Nationalist government. Although precise figures cannot be determined, it is clear that many thousands of people were slaughtered by the White Terror during the Civil War. The first indiscriminate massacres gave way to the more legalistic methods of the military tribunals set up under General Martínez Anido, who became Minister of Public Safety in the 1938 cabinet; but the killing went on unabated. Many people, conservative and Falangist alike, voiced their apprehension over the continuity of a state based on such foundations.

Martínez Anido had won his spurs as a legalized murderer by arranging the slaughter of Anarcho-Syndicalists in the great Barcelona repression of 1921–22. But that had been child's play compared to what went on after 1936. Many of the *camisas viejas* hated Martínez Anido as a reactionary and a butcher; despite their many errors of thought and deed, the Falangists had never intended the national syndicalist state to pursue a juridical policy of mass murder. In June of 1938, some of the old guard leaders proposed through Serrano Súñer that the Ministry of Public Safety be handed over to them, and that a more limited Ministry of Public Health be created for Martínez Anido. This suggestion was quietly sidestepped. Objections to the policy of brutal repression were not sufficiently widespread in influential circles to be taken seriously. When Martínez Anido died unexpectedly a few months later, Serrano Súñer took over this position as well. Serrano was still oppressed by the memory of his brothers slain in the Republican zone; the killings went on, as they would continue to do long after the Civil War had officially ended.

The full roster of the first National Council was not complete until October

19, 1937. Of its fifty members, twenty could be classified as more or less genuine Falangists; eight were Carlists, five were generals, and some seventeen were assorted monarchists, conservatives, and opportunists. This mixed fry was a good representation of the political heterogeneity behind the Franco regime. There was a sufficient variety of discordant groups to assure that nothing unplanned or original could be accomplished. The regime's favorite tactic of playing critics off against one another was already obvious. The first National Council met only a few times, and its insignificance was extreme.

Little more could be said for the party's first Junta Política. According to Serrano,

Its labors were rather insignificant, serving only to maintain official contact between the party and the state.

In some cases the meetings (it should not be forgotten that the official party, like the national movement itself, was a conglomeration of forces) were strained and even agitated. The political life of the regime resided principally in the Ministries.

The Ministries, with one exception, were controlled by non-Falangists. . . .

The overt political fusion promulgated in April 1937 reflected no real change of heart in either of the two protagonists, despite the high-sounding pronouncements of government propagandists. An order of April 30, 1937, established equal representation for each group on committees of fusion in every province, but this made little impression. Falangists and Requetés [Carlist militia] preferred to maintain separate headquarters until an order of June 8 declared that in towns with populations of less than 10,000 it was absolutely mandatory that they occupy the same quarters. Plans were also made to fuse the respective youth groups, but these were never carried out. Some veteran Carlists, as a sign of resistance, simply refused to accept FET membership cards.

However, the Requetés at the front lines reacted as did their peers in the Falange.

Rear guard politics seemed very unreal in the battle zone, but unity seemed very reasonable and very necessary. There was no interparty conflict, for too many other things required immediate attention.

Nonetheless, it was fundamentally impossible to effect a meaningful compromise between the monarchist-regionalist program of the Traditionalists and the party-minded statism of *falangismo*. Whenever the opportunity presented itself, animosity flared up in the rear lines. One French journalist asked a Falange leader what his group would do if the monarchy were really restored. The Falangist replied: "There would simply be another revolution. And this time, I assure you, we would not be on the same side." At the militia review in Burgos on October 12, 1937 (the annual "Día de la Raza"),[3] the Carlist leader, José María Zaldívar, threatened to withdraw his Requetés if they were not permitted to drill on a separate half of the field. The Requetés were not marched off, but the festive event was partially ruined by the long altercation which resulted. In the chastisement that followed, Zaldívar was expelled from the FET and several other Carlist chiefs were deprived of party rights for a period of two years.

Franco endeavored to rope in the more recalcitrant Traditionalists when he appointed Fal Conde to the National Council on November 20, 1937. A long correspondence ensued, during the course of which Fal respectfully begged off because of his opposition to "*the idea of the party* as a medium of national union, a base of the state, and an inspiration of the government, which I understand as contrary to our Traditionalist doctrine, to our antecedents, and to our very racial temperament." After Raimundo Fernández Cuesta became Secretary-General of the party in December 1937, he continued this correspondence. It ended when Fal's appoint-

[3] "Day of the Race," commemorating Columbus' discovery of America and the conquest of Mexico and most of South America by the Spaniards. [Editor's note.]

ment was finally canceled on March 6, 1938.

Initially, the Carlists had received the *jefatura provincial* in eight of the sixteen provinces of rebel Spain. According to the original understanding, such posts were to be divided evenly between the two groups, and where one received the *jefatura*, the other was to be given the *secretariado*. However, after Fernández Cuesta became Secretary of FET, the Carlists found their initiative increasingly circumscribed by the national command. After a Ministry of Syndical Organization was established at the end of January 1938, whatever influence the Carlists had achieved in syndical organization was progressively curtailed.

When Serrano Súñer became Minister of the Interior and Falange Propaganda Chief early in 1938, the Traditionalists found their propaganda activities more sharply limited than ever before. Dionisio Ridruejo and Antonio Tóvar, who directed state and party propaganda in 1938–39, were determined that national syndicalist ideology, and only national syndicalist ideology, would be expounded in the "new Spain."

The Carlists' only lasting political satisfaction was achieved . . . through the clerical laws of 1938. When the first regular Franco cabinet was set up in January of that year, Rodezno was given the portfolio of Justice, and he chose Arellano as his Subsecretary. Their main goal was to rewrite Spanish religious legislation, crushing any form of laicism, granting the Church complete educational rights, tying the state to Catholicism, and rigidly circumscribing any of the other Christian churches. With able assistance from Pedro Sáinz Rodríguez in the Ministry of Education, they were overwhelmingly successful. All opposition from the Falange was overridden, and the Jesuits were brought back to Spain within sixty days. The Carlists had finally scored a success within the Franco state, and to many of them this helped greatly to compensate for their other

frustrations. It may not have been possible to build either a Carlist or a Falangist party-state in Franco Spain, but in all ordinary civil affairs, the church-state was dominant.

Most veteran Falangists resented the overwhelming triumph of clericalism under the regime. Certain segments of the party became the last respectable strongholds of a certain brand of anticlericalism. A brawl in Seville during the autumn of 1938 between a Falange youth demonstration and a Church procession created a major scandal, which the government tried desperately to cover up.

On the civilian front, the Carlists had nothing to match the Falange's Auxilio Social,[4] set up during the first year of the war. The Carlist civilian auxiliary service of Fronts and Hospitals functioned as a part of the FET. It continued to do valiant work under Carlist leaders, but it was connected only with front-line relief; at the end of the war this service was no longer needed, and the Carlists were left with nothing. Falangist control of the social services of the FET was virtually undisputed. This meant little, however, for by late 1939 the Carlists were deserting the FET *en masse*. The evident degeneration of the party into an office-holding clique did not disillusion them, for Traditionalists had never expected anything of the Franco-Falange in the first place. At the war's end, they simply returned to the mountains they had left in the summer of 1936.

Several of the more loyal Carlist leaders were temporarily arrested or banished during the five years that followed. Fal Conde was permitted to return to Spain when the fighting ceased, but he was placed under house arrest at Seville in 1939 and was sent to internal exile at Mallorca three years later. As isolated and politically impotent as ever, the Traditionalists settled down to survive *franquismo* just as they

---

[4] The Falange social welfare organization, running hospitals, orphanages, and children's dining rooms. [Editor's note.]

had survived constitutional Monarchy and Republicanism.

The influence of Germany and Italy on the Falange during the Civil War was never more than secondary. Neither country made a direct effort to intervene in the domestic politics of rebel Spain; each feared it might affront the other if it attempted a politically aggressive policy. At first, the Italians seemed to believe that the Germans were pressing them forward in order to foist upon them any blame for overly ambitious intervention in Spain. Count Ciano informed Roberto Cantalupo, the Duce's first ambassador to Salamanca, that Italy's policy would be to avoid any kind of heavy involvement.

The Germans appeared equally diffident. On December 5, 1936, their Foreign Minister, von Neurath, defined Germany's aims as "predominantly of a commercial character." Two months earlier, Ernst von Weizsäcker, the chief political counselor at the Wilhelmstrasse, had informed the German representative that there was absolutely no authorization for them to press for a National Socialist-type revolution in Spain. The Germans never wavered from this attitude. Hassell, their ambassador in Rome, urged:

Anyone who knows the Spaniards and Spanish conditions will regard with a good deal of skepticism and also concern for future German-Spanish relations (perhaps even for German-Italian cooperation) any attempt to transplant National Socialism to Spain with German methods and German personnel. It will be easier with Latin Fascism, which is politically more formalistic; a certain aversion to the Italians on the part of the Spaniards, and their resentment of foreign leadership in general, may prove to be a hinderance, but that is a matter for the Italians to cope with.

The Italians demonstrated a complete disinclination to cope with it. They had little interest in or acumen for Spanish politics, and they had never shown any great confidence in the future of Iberian fascism.

The only foreign "intervention" of any sort that took place in Salamanca occurred during the spring of 1937. In the months immediately preceding the unification, Faupel had feared that the military dictatorship would discard the fascist party before it even got started. In January 1937 he had written:

The Government believes at present that by taking over part of the Falange program it can carry out social reforms even without the Falange itself. This is possible. But it is not possible without the cooperation of the Falange to imbue the Spanish workers, especially those in the Red territory to be conquered, with national and really practicable social ideas and to win them over to the new state. For that reason collaboration between the Government and the Falange is still indispensable.

As has been seen, Faupel urged both Hedilla and the Generalissimo to work for political unification and the formation of a revolutionary state party. However, this encouragement never went beyond conversations arranged on the very personal initiative of the German ambassador. Faupel fully realized that the Army was the basic power in rebel Spain; he admitted that it would be impossible to back the party if it ever tried to back the Army:

If in his attempt to bring the parties together Franco should meet with opposition from the Falange, we and the Italians are agreed that, in spite of all our inclination toward the Falange and its sound tendencies, we must support Franco, who after all intends to make the program of the Falange the basis of his internal policy. The realization of the most urgently needed social reforms is possible only with Franco, not in opposition to him.

Faupel was not pleased by the results of the April *diktat* and greatly distrusted the "reactionaries" in Salamanca. As previously mentioned, he pressed the Caudillo for leniency in dealing with Hedilla, but his request for a formal protest was denied by the German Foreign Office. In return, both Franco and Serrano came to detest Faupel for his officiousness and gratuitous counsel, even though the German ambassador seems at first to have trusted in the sincerity of the *cuñadísimo*. When he tried to foist on Fermín Yzurdiaga, FET Chief of Press and Propaganda, a plan for a German-directed propaganda and information-exchange institute to be named for Charles V, the Caudillo's annoyance increased. Faupel was finally recalled in October 1937.

Dr. Eberhard von Stohrer, his successor, was more congenial to the rebel leaders. The new ambassador emphasized that Germany should avoid "any interference in Spanish domestic affairs."

We have thus far confined ourselves to indicating our particular sympathies for that movement in the Falange which is called the "original Falange," the "revolutionary Falange," or the "Camisas viejas," which is closest to us ideologically and whose aims, in our opinion, also offer Spain the best guaranty for the establishment of a new and strong national state which could be useful to us. We have, therefore, readily placed our experience at the disposal of the Falange, have shown our party organizations, social institutions, etc., in Germany to picked representatives of the Falange, and have advised them upon request. We have thereby considerably lightened their task here, but we have naturally not been able to strengthen them to the extent that the victory of this element is assured.

The Falangists naturally felt strongly sympathetic to the German and Italian parties. There was considerable propaganda interchange and the Falange organized pro-German "galas." Many of the first leaders of the party's Auxilio Social were sent to Germany for training in the Winterhilfe [Winter Aid]. That, however, was the limit:

On request, the Falange receives from the German press office a wealth of material on German conditions and the organization, etc., of the NSDAP [initials of the Nazi Party]. There is no importunate propaganda or "intervention in the internal affairs" of Spain. Any objection of this type formerly made can at most refer to the beginnings of the Falange (the Hedilla affair).

In Berlin, neither the ambition nor the interest of Nazi leaders was aroused by the Falange. Dionisio Ridruejo recalls that the party was never mentioned on either of the two trips he made to Germany, in 1937 and in 1940. During the spring of 1938 Weizsäcker wrote that it no longer seemed worth while to attempt to cultivate the Falange as an independent entity.

Many of the party's foreign connections depended on Serrano Súñer in the period following unification. His Catholic conservation drew him more toward the Italian Fascist Party than toward the Nazis, but the Italians took little interest in Spanish internal developments. They had not even a consistent foreign policy. Mussolini could not bring himself to risk a heavy involvement in Spain until the resounding defeat of the Italian expeditionary force at Guadalajara in March 1937. By that time, the Duce was so confused about the real facts of Spanish affairs, misinformed as he was by groups of mutually suspicious intriguers, that he sent Roberto Farinacci on a formal mission to Salamanca; according to his military attaché, Farinacci's main task was to gather accurate information.

A secondary political objective of this mission was to sound out the willingness of Spanish authorities to accept a proposed Italian candidate for the Spanish throne. Such a regime would supposedly be set up with the Falange playing the role of the Italian Fascist Party. However, independently of each other, both Franco and Hedilla rejected this scheme, and it was quickly forgotten.

Immediately following the unification, Signor Danzi, the Italian Fascist Party's representative at Salamanca, offered a copy of his party's statutes to the Caudillo, so that they might be used as a model for the FET. As the German ambassador predicted, these were largely ignored. After that, the Italians seemed to lose interest altogether. They left the FET and its masters quite alone.

When Dionisio Ridruejo accompanied Serrano Súñer on a state visit to Rome in the summer of 1938, he was drawn aside by Ciano and asked which men were of present or potential importance in the Spanish party. Ridruejo replied, "Either Serrano Súñer or Fernández Cuesta." Ciano then closed the matter by saying that the ex-Cedista FET members he had seen reminded him of the elderly, conservative wing of the old Partito Popolare. He indicated that he considered it impossible to build a real fascist party with such material.

A year later, after visiting Spain, Ciano changed his attitude:

The central factor in the country is now the Falange. It is a party which is still only beginning to build up its formation and activity [on the contrary, it was already on the downgrade], but it already has grouped around it the youth, the most active elements, and in particular the women [evidently referring to the special labors of Auxilio Social and the Sección Femenina].

However, Ciano's more positive estimation of the Spanish party came long after Franco and Serrano Súñer had made the Falange their own. The principle of non-intervention in Franco's domestic affairs was already well established, and the Falange would henceforth reflect only those characteristics of the Italian party that were desired by the Caudillo. During the crucial months in Salamancan politics, neither Germany nor Italy had been able to arouse herself for a serious effort at intervention. Italian suspicion, German disinclination, and the mutual hesitation of both nations prevented them from seeking political castles in Spain. Francisco Franco, the only man who ever outplayed Hitler, was left to build his peculiar little system unhindered.

SUGGESTIONS FOR ADDITIONAL READING

To begin with I should state that all the books from which selections appear in this anthology are worth reading in their entirety. On the wider background of Spanish problems, Rafael Altamira, *A History of Spain* (New York, 1949) offers an accurate, though not too interestingly written, one-volume survey. F. G. Bruguera, *Histoire contemporaine de l'Espagne* (Paris, 1953) contains a great deal of important economic and demographic information from the year 1789 forward. Salvador de Madariaga, *Spain* (New York, 1958) illuminates the period from roughly 1875 on but is rather arbitrary and idiosyncratic in its emphases. Two very brief incisive interpretations of Spanish history are Pierre Vilar, *Histoire de l'Espagne* (Paris, 1947) and Jaime Vicens Vives, *Aproximación a la historia de España* (Barcelona, 1952). José Ortega y Gasset, *Invertebrate Spain* (New York, 1937) is a classic concerning the political psychology of the Spaniards. Américo Castro, *The Structure of Spanish History* (Princeton, 1954) is an invaluable aid to the understanding of Spain, though many of its specific propositions are open to question.

Several works which make clear the intellectual ferment at work in modern Spain, particularly Krausism and liberalism, are J. B. Trend, *The Origins of Modern Spain* (Cambridge, England, 1934); Pierre Jobit, *Les éducateurs de l'Espagne moderne* (Paris, 1936); José López Morillas, *El Krausismo español* (Mexico, D.F., 1956); Jean Sarrailh, *L'Espagne éclairée de la seconde moitié du XVIIIe siècle* (Paris, 1954); and Richard Herr, *The Eighteenth Century Revolution in Spain* (Princeton, 1958). The weaknesses of the First Republic of 1873 are clearly chronicled in Joseph A. Brandt, *Towards the New Spain* (Chicago, 1933) and C. A. M. Hennessey, *The Federal Republic in Spain* (Oxford, 1962). Worthwhile studies of the major regional questions are the two works of Maximiano

García Venero, *Historia del nacionalismo catalan* (Madrid, 1944) and *Historia del nacionalismo vasco* (Madrid, 1945). Fundamental for understanding the social conflicts and the influence of anarchism are Juan Díaz del Moral, *Historia de las agitaciones campesinas andaluzas-Córdoba* (Madrid, 1929) and Joan Connelly, *The Tragic Week: a Study of Anticlericalism in Spain* (Ann Arbor, University Microfilms, 1964). Important also for understanding the clerical issue is E. Allison Peers, *Spain, the Church, and the Orders* (London, 1939). There is a great deal of good history, and especially there is masterful portrayal of the political psychology of the Spaniards in the historical novels of Benito Pérez Galdós, known collectively as the *Episodios Nacionales*.

The most detailed general history of the Second Republic is the four volume work of José Plá, *Historia de la segunda república española* (Barcelona, 1940–41). This book, and the single volume history by Melchor Fernández Almagro, *Historia de la república española* (Madrid, 1940) are strictly political chronicles and offer almost no economic and social information. They are objective in tone, but like all works published in Spain since the Civil War, they emphasize the disorders and uncertainties of the Republican era. Joaquín Arrarás, *Historia de la segunda república española* (Madrid, 1956) is the first volume of a projected multi-volume history. Even more than the earlier cited works it emphasizes parliamentary squabbling, public "disorder," and the pained disillusionment of the military with the Republic. A useful summary of these years by an American political scientist of liberal sympathies is Frank E. Manuel, *The Politics of Modern Spain* (New York, 1938). Both the ideals and the program of the Republic were personified by Manuel Azaña, the volumes of whose collected speeches therefore constitute a historical source of the highest importance.

I list their titles in chronological order rather than alphabetical sequence: *Una política* (Madrid, 1932), *En el poder y en la oposición* (Madrid, 1934), *Mi rebelión en Barcelona* (Madrid, 1935), and *Discursos en campo abierto* (Madrid, 1936).

There are several important works dealing with specific aspects of the Republic. Rhea Marsh Smith, *The Day of the Liberals in Spain* (Philadelphia, 1938) provides a detailed history of the formation of the constitution of 1931. Jules Moch and Germaine Picard-Moch, *L'Espagne républicaine* (Paris, 1933) is a very perceptive work by French Socialists who had many personal contacts with national and local leaders of the Republican-Socialist coalition. Pascual Carrión, *Los latifundios en España* (Madrid, 1932) is an excellent technical study which greatly influenced the writing of agrarian reform legislation. Alfredo Mendizábal, *The Martyrdom of Spain* (London, 1937) is the work of a liberal Catholic law professor who emphasizes the errors and responsibilities of the Church as well as the crimes of which it was the victim. Anton Sieberer, *Katalonien gegen Kastilien* (Vienna, 1936), published also as *Espagne contre Espagne* (Geneva, 1937) summarizes ably the role of Catalan nationalism during the Republican era. Lawrence Fernsworth, *Spain's Struggle for Freedom* (Boston, 1957) offers much interesting information on both the clerical and Catalan questions. During the Republic Fernsworth was a liberal Catholic journalist stationed in Barcelona. A first biography of Azaña in English is Frank Sedwick, *The Tragedy of Manuel Azaña* (Columbus, Ohio, 1963). An evocative autobiography of the time is Constancia de la Mora, *In Place of Splendor* (New York, 1939). The author was the Republican and feminist daughter of the very conservative and aristocratic Maura family. Eduardo Comín Colomer, *Historia secreta de la segunda república* (Barcelona, 1959) is important as a work which is used in the education of police and military officers. It interprets the Republic as an international Masonic-Jewish-Communist plot.

The best general histories of the Civil War, covering both political and military, national and international aspects, are Pierre Broué and Emile Témime, *La révolution et la guerre d'Espagne* (Paris, 1961) and Julián Zugazagoitia, *Historia de la guerra en España* (Buenos Aires, 1940). Hugh Thomas, *The Spanish Civil War* (London and New York, 1961) includes much important military and diplomatic information, but is inaccurate and misleading with regard to the Spanish context. The finest single book dealing with foreign intervention is P.A.M. Van der Esch, *Prelude to War* (The Hague, 1951). An excellent political-military study of one phase of the war is Robert G. Colodny, *The Struggle for Madrid* (New York, 1958). The rise of the Communists and the fall of Largo Caballero are excellently documented in Burnett Bolloten, *The Grand Camouflage* (London, 1961). Ramón Serrano Súñer, *Entre Hendaya y Gibraltar* (Madrid, 1947) is the work of General Franco's brother-in-law and close wartime adviser, and is essential to any study of the early years of Nationalist rule. Several Spanish participants wrote important memoirs which are available in English. Antonio Ruiz Vilaplana, *Burgos Justice* (New York, 1938) deals with the first months of the war behind the lines in the Nationalist zone. The wartime Foreign Minister of the Republic, Julio Alvarez del Vayo, in *Freedom's Battle* (New York, 1940) deals with the Civil War, and in *The Last Optimist* (New York, 1949) deals with phases both of the war and its antecedents. Two Republican staff officers have left circumstantial accounts of the war: José Martín Blázquez, *I Helped to Build an Army* (London, 1939) and Segismundo Casado, *The Last Days of Madrid* (London, 1939). There are two very important works on the role of the Church. Juan de Iturralde (pseudonym of the exiled Basque priest Juan de Usabiaga), *El catoli-*

cismo y la cruzada de Franco, two volumes (Vienne, France, 1955 and 1960) documents the reactionary and anti-regionalist tendencies of the Church in the 1930's. Antonio Montero, *Historia de la persecución religiosa en España, 1936–1939* (Madrid, 1961) studies in detail the destruction of both life and property suffered by the Church during the war. Franz Borkenau, *The Spanish Cockpit* (Ann Arbor, 1963) contains valuable eyewitness accounts of anarchist activities in peace and war.

There is a large and fascinating literature on the International Brigades. Among the best works are Alvah Bessie, *Men in Battle* (New York, 1939); Marcel Acier, editor, *From Spanish Trenches* (New York, 1937), a collection of letters by Internationals; Luigi Longo, *Le Brigate internationali in Spagna* (Rome, 1956), published also in German as *Die internationalen brigaden in Spanien* (Berlin, 1958) by a leading Italian Communist; Ludwig Renn (pseudonym of A. F. Vieth von Golssenau) *Der Spanische Krieg* (Berlin, 1956) by a German Communist intellectual who had been a professional officer in the World War I German Army; and Pietro Nenni, *Spagna* (Rome, 1958), published in French as *La guerre d'Espagne* (Paris, 1960) by the Italian Left Socialist leader who was an officer in the International Brigades.

There is much interesting information on both politics and diplomacy in the book by the American ambassador to Spain: Claude G. Bowers, *My Mission to Spain* (New York, 1954). Some of the finest war journalism appears in two books by the New York Times correspondent Herbert L. Matthews: *Two Wars and More to Come* (New York, 1938) and *The Education of a Correspondent* (New York, 1946). There are some important chapters concerning Spain in Pierre Cot, *The Triumph of Treason* (New York, 1941); Louis Fischer, *Men and Politics* (New York, 1941); Reynolds and Eleanor Packard, *Balcony Empire* (New York, 1942); and Vincent

Sheean, *Not Peace but a Sword* (New York, 1939). The sections devoted to the Spanish Civil War in the Royal Institute *Survey of International Affairs* for the years 1937 and 1938 remain among the best English accounts. An important recent study of the international power politics of the Civil War is Dante Puzzo, *Spain and the Great Powers, 1936–1941* (New York, 1963). The role of Mexico as the one power consistently supporting the rights of the Republican government is examined in Lois Elwyn Smith, *Mexico and the Spanish Republicans* (Berkeley, 1955). Legal aspects of neutrality, the League of Nations attitude, and the work of the Non-Intervention Committee are treated in Norman J. Padelford, *International Law and Diplomacy in the Spanish Civil Strife* (New York, 1939). Soviet diplomacy is thoroughly analyzed in David T. Cattell, *Soviet Diplomacy and the Spanish Civil War* (Berkeley, 1957). The activities and the judgments of German, and to a lesser extent, Italian, diplomats are laid before the reader in the U.S. government publication: *Documents on German Foreign Policy, 1918–1945,* Series D, vol. iii, "Germany and the Spanish Civil War," Washington, 1950.

The political and economic development of the Franco regime are treated in Thomas J. Hamilton, *Appeasement's Child, the Franco Regime in Spain* (New York, 1943); Herbert Feis, *The Spanish Story* (New York, 1948); Herbert L. Matthews, *The Yoke and the Arrows* (New York, 1957); and E. Allison Peers, *Spain in Eclipse* (London, 1943). The heavy legacy of spiritual, political, and social problems bequeathed by the Civil War are acutely analyzed in Eléna de La Souchère, *Explanation of Spain* (New York, 1963) and Carlos M. Rama, *La crisis española del siglo XX* (Mexico, D.F., 1960). Several works of particular interest from a United States point of view are: F. Jay Taylor, *The United States and the Spanish Civil War* (New York, 1956) which treats in detail the neutrality policy, the variations of public and congressional opinion, and the actions of various pressure groups; Allen Guttman, *The Wound in the Heart* (Glencoe, Illinois, 1962), which deals with the attitudes of intellectuals, writers, and opinion-forming leaders of the business and professional world; and Carleton J. H. Hayes, *Wartime Mission in Spain, 1942–1945* (New York, 1945). Hayes was a distinguished historian who served as first U.S. ambassador to Franco Spain.

Finally, there have been numerous works of fiction, the best of which contribute greatly to a psychological understanding of Spain and the Civil War. Ernest Hemingway, *For Whom the Bell Tolls* (New York, 1940) illuminated the motives of both Spanish guerrillas and Internationals. André Malraux, *Man's Hope* (New York, 1938) gives a vivid picture of anarchist psychology and of street actions in Barcelona. Gustav Regler, *The Great Crusade* (New York, 1940) epitomizes the hopes and the role of the German and Italian anti-fascist Internationals. Ramón Sender, in *Seven Red Sundays* (London, 1936) and in many other novels and stories available in Spanish, interprets the war as a Spanish left-liberal. José Gironella, in *The Cypresses Believe in God* (New York, 1956) and *One Million Dead* (New York, 1963) has portrayed the war from a conservative, disabused point of view. Dario Puccini, editor, *Le romancero de la résistance espagnole* (Paris, 1962) brings together hundreds of poems by Spaniards and foreigners who espoused the cause of the Republic.